IN THE PENINSULA WITH A FRENCH HUSSAR

LINES OF TORRES VEDRAS

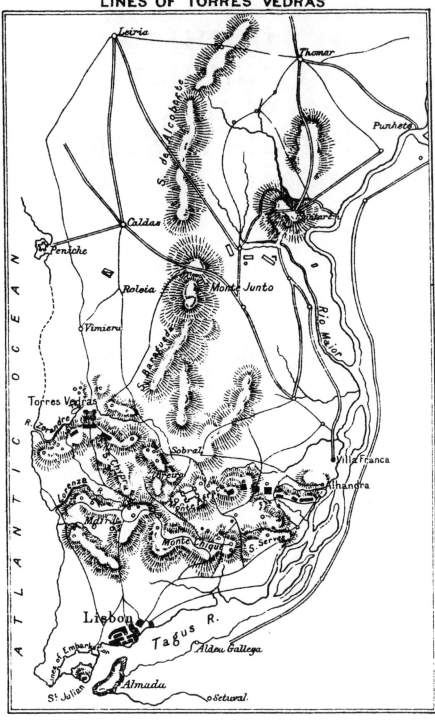

IN THE PENINSULA WITH A FRENCH HUSSAR

MEMOIRS OF THE WAR OF THE FRENCH IN SPAIN

Albert Jean Michel de Rocca

Introduction by Philip Haythornthwaite

Frontline Books

In the Peninsula with a French Hussar

A Greenhill Book
First published in 1990 by Greenhill Books, Lionel Leventhal Limited
www.greenhillbooks.com

This edition published in 2017 by

Frontline Books
an imprint of Pen & Sword Books Ltd,
47 Church Street, Barnsley, S. Yorkshire, S70 2AS
For more information on our books, please visit
www.frontline-books.com, email info@frontline-books.com
or write to us at the above address.

This edition © Lionel Leventhal Limited, 1990
Introduction © Philip Haythornthwaite, 1990

ISBN: 978-1-47388-261-4

Publishing History
In the Peninsula with a French Hussar was first published in Paris in 1814 as
Mémoires sur la Guerre des Français en Espagne. This edition presents, complete
and unabridged, the entire text of the first English language edition, translated by
Maria Graham, published in London, 1815, (John Murray). A new Introduction
by Philip Haythornthwaite has been added to this edition, plus maps.

CIP data records for this title are available from the British Library

Printed and bound by CPI Group (UK) Ltd, Croydon, CR0 4YY

CHRONOLOGY OF THE PENINSULAR WAR
(entries involving de Rocca in italics)

1807:	18 October	Junot crosses the Bidassoa
	30 November	Junot enters Lisbon
1808:	9 February	Duhesme enters Catalonia
	2 May	Insurrection in Madrid
	15 June–17 August	First siege of Saragossa, ending in French withdrawal
	14 July	Battle of Medina del Rio Seco: Bessières defeats Cuesta
	19 July	Battle of Baylen: Dupont defeated by Castaños
	8 August	Disembarkation of British expeditionary force in Portugal
	17 August	Battle of Roliça (or Roleia): Wellesley defeats Delaborde
	21 August	Battle of Vimeiro: Wellesley defeats Junot
	22 August	Convention of Cintra between Junot and British allows French to quit Portugal
	September	*2nd Hussars leave Prussia to go to Spain*
	9 November	Capture of Burgos by Soult
	10 November	*2nd Hussars march into Burgos*
	23 November	Battle of Tudela: Lannes defeats Castaños
	30 November	Battle of Somosierra: Napoleon defeats San Juan
	5 December	*2nd Hussars reviewed by Napoleon*
	19 December	*2nd Hussars form part of garrison of Madrid*
	20 December–20 February 1809	Second siege of Saragossa, ending in French victory
	21 December	Paget defeats Debelle at Sahagun
	29 December	Paget defeats Lefebvre-Desnouëttes at Benevente

5

1809: 3 January   Action at Cacabelos in which French general Colbert is killed in skirmish with Moore's rearguard

         13 January   *2nd Hussars leave Madrid*

         16 January   Battle of Corunna: Moore defeats Soult; Moore is killed and his army is evacuated

         16 March   Action at Almaraz: Victor defeats Cuesta

         28 March   Soult captures Oporto

         28 March   *Battle of Medellin: Victor defeats Cuesta*

         12 May   Action at Oporto: Wellesley defeats Soult and French evacuate Portugal

         20 May   *De Rocca ordered from Spain to return home to recruit; then sent to Flanders as a result of the British expedition to Walcheren*

         4 June–11 December   Siege of Gerona, ending in French victory

         28 July   Battle of Talavera: Wellesley defeats Victor

         19 November   Battle of Ocaña: Soult defeats Areizago

         Late 1809–early 1810   *De Rocca returns to Spain*

1810: *22 January*   *De Rocca skirmishes with Porliere's Spanish guerrillas*

         16 March   *De Rocca engaged in heavy skirmish with guerrillas near Campillos*

         1 May   *De Rocca wounded in guerrilla ambush near Ronda*

         6 June–10 July   Siege of Ciudad Rodrigo; city captured by the French

         22 June   *De Rocca leaves Ronda to begin convalescence*

         24 July   Action on River Coa: Ney engages Craufurd

         End July   *De Rocca leaves Spain*

         15–27 August   Siege of Almeida; city captured by Massena

         27 September   Battle of Busaco: Wellington defeats Massena

         9 October–March 1811   Massena halted by Lines of Torres Vedras; he retires after his army starves during the winter

1811: 27 January–11 March   Siege of Badajoz; city captured by the French

         4 March   Battle of Barossa: Graham defeats Victor

         16 March   Action at Foz d'Arouce: Wellington pursues French

         3 April   Action at Sabugal: Wellington defeats Reynier

         5 May   Battle of Fuentes de Oñoro: Wellington defeats Massena

         16 May   Battle of Albuera: Beresford defeats Soult

	24 May–28 June	Siege of Tarragona: city captured by Suchet
	14 June	Action at Sanguesa: Caffarelli defeats Mina's guerrillas
	22 June	Action at Cifuentes: Hugo defeats guerrillas of 'El Empecinado' (Juan Diaz)
	1 October	Action at Tarifa: British repulse French
	28 October	Battle of Arroyo dos Molinos: Hill defeats Girard
	26 December–9 January 1812	Siege of Valencia: city captured by Suchet
1812:	19 January	Siege of Ciudad Rodrigo ends with Wellington's capture of city
	16 March–6 April	Siege of Badajoz: city captured by Wellington
	22 July	Battle of Salamanca: Wellington defeats Marmont
	13 August	Wellington enters Madrid
	19 September	Siege of Burgos: Wellington abandons the siege and retires
	2 November	French re-enter Madrid
1813:	12 June	French abandon Madrid
	21 June	Battle of Vittoria: Wellington defeats Joseph and Jourdan
	25 July	Action at Roncesvalles and Maya: Wellington defeats Soult
	28–30 July	Action at Sorauren: Wellington defeats Soult
	31 August	Capture of San Sebastian by Wellington
	9 November	Action at St. Jean de Luz: Hope defeats Soult
	10 November	Battle of Nivelle: Wellington defeats Soult
	9–12 December	Battle of Nive: Wellington defeats Soult
	13 December	Action at St. Pierre: Hill defeats Soult
1814:	27 February	Battle of Orthez: Wellington defeats Soult
	10 April	Battle of Toulouse: Wellington defeats Soult
	14 April	Action at Bayonne: Hope repels French sortie from the city

INTRODUCTION

by

Philip Haythornthwaite

The war in the Iberian Peninsula began in 1807 when Napoleon sent an army through Spain and into Portugal, in an attempt to compel the latter country to close its harbours to British goods, as part of his 'continental system' designed to ruin British trade. Following this foray into Portugal, Napoleon deposed the ineffectual Spanish royal family and installed his own brother Joseph as king. This was the trigger for a widespread uprising by the Spanish population, which grew into a guerrilla war of very considerable proportion, led by guerrilla chieftains like Francisco Espoz y Mina, the eccentrically-named 'El Empecinado' ('Inky Face': Juan Martin Diaz), and Juan Porlier, alias 'El Marquesito', who appears in these pages.

Contrasting with the ineffectual nature of the official Spanish military forces, the guerrilla war was waged with vigour by the Spanish population and with intense brutality on either side, massacre and counter-atrocity being commonplace. Although the most familiar aspects of the war are the operations of the Anglo-Portuguese army under Sir Arthur Wellesley, later 1st Duke of Wellington, which eventually drove the French from the Peninsula, the spasmodic guerrilla war was of crucial significance in occupying the attention of huge numbers of French troops throughout the country, operations which according to one estimate cost the French as many as one hundred men per day during the war, the 'Spanish ulcer', as Napoleon called it, which eventually bled his army dry.

It was into this guerrilla war that Sous-Lieutenant Albert Jean Michel de Rocca entered in 1808. He came from one of the most distinguished families of Geneva, third son of Jean-François Rocca who, as a member of the senate, was one of the leading citizens of his country. Albert Jean Michel – known as 'Little John' in his youth – was more adventurous

8

than his Calvinist background might have suggested, and in 1805 he
enlisted in Napoleon's cavalry, following a long tradition of service by
Swiss soldiers in the French army, which probably reached the peak of
its fame in the Napoleonic army. The regiment in which he served in
Spain was one of the most distinguished in the army, the 2nd Hussars,
which, despite the deliberate eradication for political reasons of 'noble'
titles in the early French republican period, still maintained
(unofficially and doubtless for reasons of regimental tradition and
esprit de corps) its old name, Chamborant, by which name de Rocca
himself refers to his regiment.

Raised at Strasbourg in 1734 by Count Esterhazy, the regiment took
the name Chamborant from its colonel in 1761; the colour of its uniform, a most distinctive chestnut-brown with sky-blue facings and
breeches, was reputedly suggested by Marie Antoinette who remarked
upon the colour of the habit of a passing monk when Chamborant
asked what colour she would suggest for the uniform of his regiment. It
is interesting to note that the colour of this uniform, very unusual in the
French army, may well have saved de Rocca's life, by causing hostile
Spanish peasants to mistake him for a member of their own forces.

Entering Spain after their campaign against Prussia, the 2nd Hussars
distinguished themselves especially at the battle of Medellin, and continued to serve in that country throughout the war. They fought at
Talavera, but their most famous exploit was probably the charge at
Albuera, executed in conjunction with the Lancers of the Vistula
Legion, which caught Colborne's British brigade before it could form
square and virtually annihilated three of its four battalions; the 2nd
also suffered heavily in this famous action, sustaining 73 casualties
among its 23 officers and 282 other ranks. Much of the regiment's
service was spent in anti-guerrilla operations, though it was present
against Wellington at Vittoria (where it was almost unengaged) and at
Toulouse, the final battle of the war. Albert Jean Michel de Rocca
served at Medellin, but missed Talavera because of being sent home,
originally to recruit and later to oppose the British expedition to
Walcheren; and ten months before Albuera, he was invalided from the
regiment following severe injury in a skirmish with guerrillas some
months after his return in Spain.

It was following this injury that de Rocca wrote his account of his
service in Spain, published in 1814 as *Mémoires sur la Guerre des
Français en Espagne*, which presumably was completed around the
early summer of 1811, as the last action he mentions is that at Foz de
Arouce (often, as here, mis-spelled 'Foz de Aronce'), with revisions,
especially of statistics, and a final paragraph added at a later date,
noting the resistance to France made by Russia and Prussia in 1812–14.

The text in this book is that of the first English edition (1815), to which a few explanatory notes might be useful. The Prince of Neufchâtel to whom de Rocca refers (by his Swiss title) is more familiar as Marshal Louis-Alexandre Berthier (1753–1815); de Rocca's 'Cenarmont' is General Alexandre Sénarmont (1769–1810), the famous artillery commander later killed by a shell during the siege of Cadiz; and the 'General Lefêvre' who was captured at Benevente is General Charles Lefebvre-Desnouëttes (1773–1822). Not unnaturally, this first English translation uses contemporary English military terms, so that 'flank companies' are mentioned, an appellation not used in French service but signifying what the French styled 'élite companies'; riflemen are also mentioned, but although the function of the French troops styled *voltigeurs* and *tirailleurs* was like that of the British rifle corps, the French did not carry rifled muskets and thus the use of the term may be slightly misleading.

It is especially interesting to note de Rocca's remark that his residence in England allowed him to procure details which were not available on the continent, such as accurate statistics of strengths and casualties. French despatches were notoriously (and often deliberately) inaccurate, giving rise to the expression 'to lie like a bulletin'; whereas the statistics published in Britain were generally as accurate as it was possible to be. De Rocca's mention of the British casualties at Busaco is a case in point: presumably he took his figure of 1,235 from Wellington's despatch published in the *London Gazette* on 15 October 1810, where 1,253 casualties are listed, de Rocca or the typesetter accidentally transposing the last two digits. Care should be taken with contemporary opinions, however: for example, Moore appears to have lost less than 6,000 men in the retreat to Corunna, rather than the 10,000 claimed by de Rocca.

Following de Rocca's return to France after his injury, French fortunes in the Peninsula declined. Wellington husbanded his initially meagre forces (de Rocca calls him 'that modern Fabius', an apposite analogy to the esteemed and cautious Roman general Quintus Fabius Maximus, alias 'Cunctator') until he was eventually able to drive the French back over the Pyrenees. The guerrillas constantly harried the French occupation forces, cutting communications and massacring stragglers, 'like avenging vultures eager for prey' as de Rocca so appropriately describes. Assailed from all sides in a hostile and inhospitable country, the French troops came to hate the war in Spain; de Rocca speaks for the army when he remarks that the Peninsular War ruined France 'without even interesting the military honour of the nation', and that he 'was glad, at any price, to quit an unjust and inglorious war, where the sentiments of my heart continually disavowed the evil my arm was condemned to do'.

Having recovered from his wounds but still on crutches, de Rocca returned to Geneva, where he met and became infatuated with the famous Madame de Staël (Anne Louise Germaine Necker, Baronne de Staël-Holstein). This society hostess, daughter of the former Bourbon finance mininster, Jacques Necker (1732–1804), was one of the greatest literary personalities of the age, and so steadfast in her opposition to Napoleon that she was banished from France as a result, and established a new circle at Coppet in Switzerland, her father's estate at Lake Geneva. Despite the disparity in their ages – de Rocca was 23 and Madame de Staël 45 – the young hussar fell madly in love, to the extent that despite his injuries he challenged to a duel the lady's former favourite, the writer and politician Henri Benjamin Constant de Rebecque (1767–1830). The duel was called off, but de Rocca continued to harass his supposed rival until he left the country.

In May 1811 de Rocca and Madame de Staël participated in a formal ceremony of betrothal, and left Switzerland to escape completely from Napoleon's sphere of influence; they travelled to Vienna, St Petersburg and Stockholm, and thence to England, where Madame de Staël was lionized during the 1813 season. A few months after their betrothal Madame de Staël had become pregnant, which caused her considerable embarrassment but gave de Rocca much pleasure, although their relationship was only formally legalized by marriage shortly before her death. Their son was born in frail health, and Madame de Staël insisted that he was raised by foster parents. They were in Paris when Napoleon returned from Elba for his 'Hundred Days', and they fled to Coppet until Napoleon was defeated at Waterloo. In October they set out for Italy, for the benefit of de Rocca's health: he was dying of consumption. Despite Madame de Staël's ill-health, in June 1816 they returned to Coppet, and then to Paris; she died on 14 June 1817. De Rocca survived her by little more than six months.

P.H.
1990

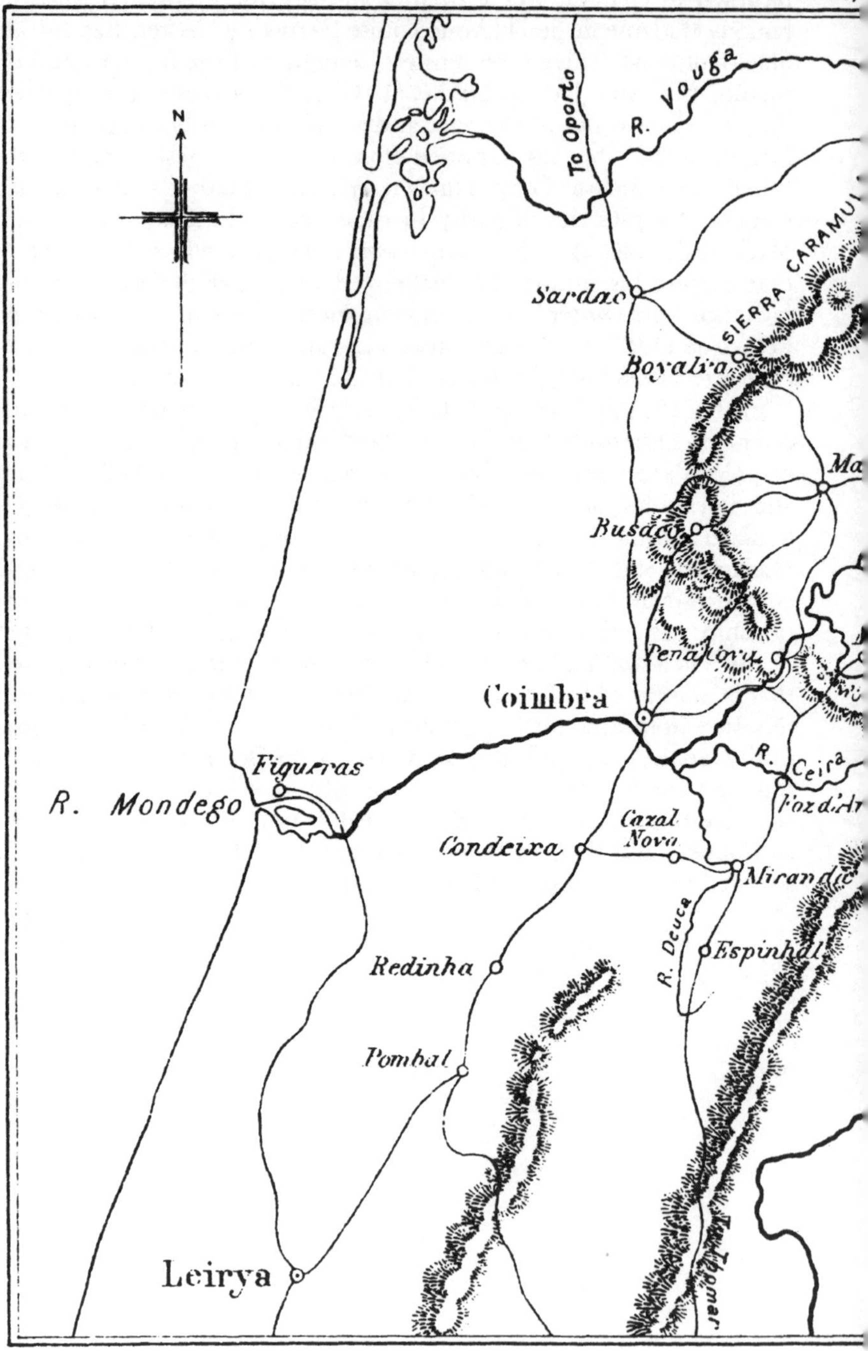

N

To Oporto

R. Vouga

SIERRA CARAMUL

Sardao

Boyalra

Ma

Busaco

Penaliru

Coimbra

R. Ceira

Figueras

Foz d'Ar

R. Mondego

Cazal
Nova

Condeixa

Mirandic

R. Deuca

Redinha

Espinhal

Pombal

Tomar

Leirya

To Lamego

To Pinhel and Almeida

Visen

Fornos

Celorico

Macal

Guarda

R. Mondego

R. Alvs

SIERRA ESTRELLA

Belmonte

To Sabugal

Castel Branco

R. Ponsul

Sobriera Formosa

English Miles

10   5   0   10

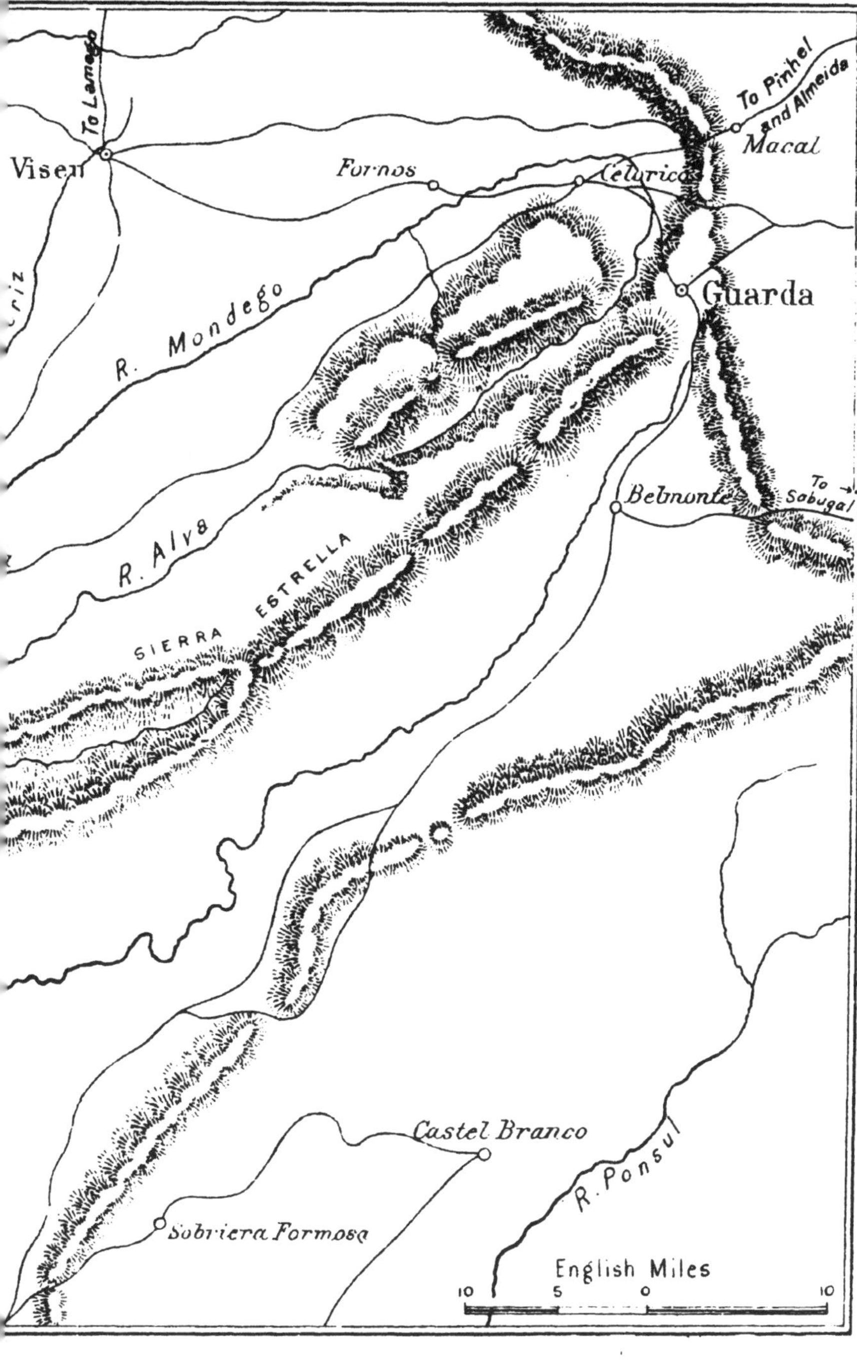

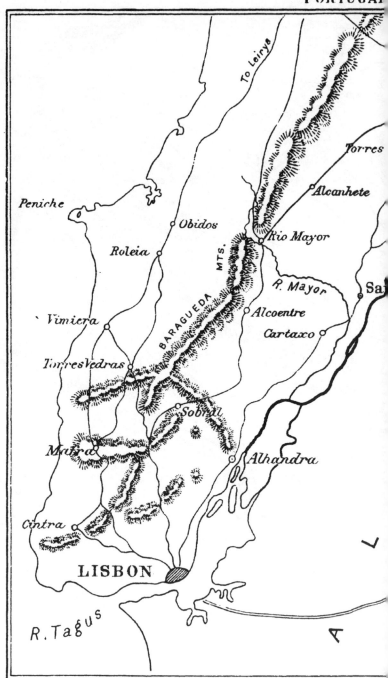

To Leirya

Peniche

Obidos

Roleia

Vimiera

Torres Vedras

Mafra

Cintra

LISBON

R. Tagus

Torres

Alcanhete

Rio Mayor

BARAGUEDA MTS.

R. Mayor

Sa

Alcoentre

Cartaxo

Sobral

Alhandra

A

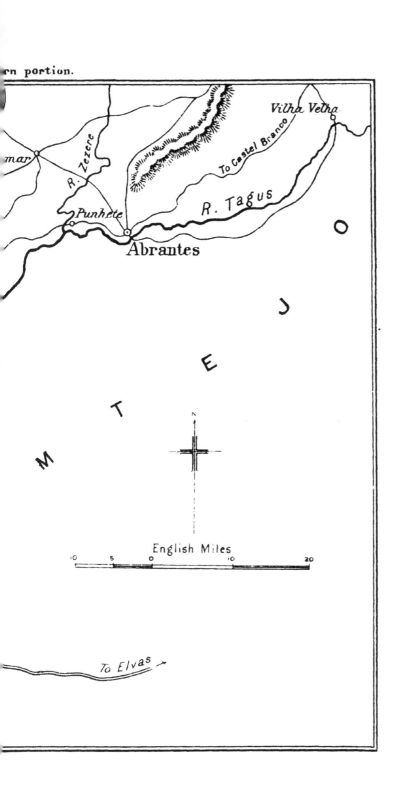

English Miles

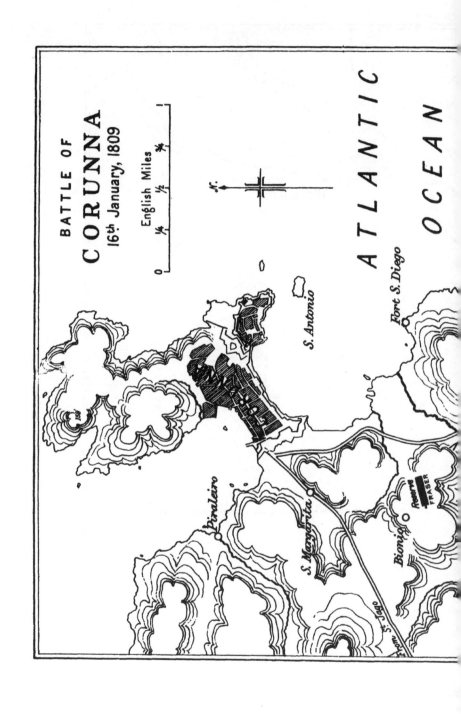

BATTLE OF
CORUNNA
16th January, 1809

English Miles

0   ¼   ½   ¾   1

N.

S. Antonio

Piraleiro

S. Margarita

Bionio

Reserve
FRASER

Fort S. Diego

From S.t Jago

ATLANTIC

OCEAN

River Mero or Burgo

Portillo

Scicho

El Burgo

Passage

Lugo

Villaboa

Cambre

Reserve

PAGET

Airis

Monte Mero

HOPE

Spot where Moore Fell

Prenalonga

Mero

Portlonga

Hts of Palavea

Palavea Abaxo

Elvina

BAIRD

Hts of Penasquedo

Rock & Height

S. Cristobal

Heights of S. Cristobal

Allies ....
French ....

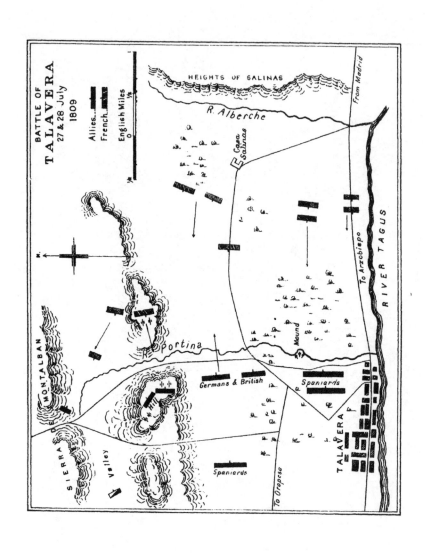

FIRST PART

I

THE SECOND regiment of hussars, formerly called Chamboran, in which I had the honour to serve, received orders to quit Prussia in order to go to Spain the year the year after the campaign which was terminated by the battle of Friedland and the peace of Tilsit. I thus found myself placed in a situation to compare two kinds of war absolutely different: the war of regular troops, commonly little interested in the object of the quarrel they maintain; and the war of resistance which a nation can oppose to regular conquering armies.

We were called from the sandy plains of the north of Germany; we had had to do with people, subject, for the most part, to governments whose forms were entirely military. The different sovereigns who made up the parts of the Germanic body had, for more than a century, turned all their views towards perfecting those military institutions which might secure their authority and serve their personal ambition; but in accustoming their subjects to a minutely punctual obedience, they had weakened the national character, the only invincible bulwark that nations can oppose to foreign invaders.

When a province of Germany was conquered by the French, and could no longer receive the orders of its sovereign, the inferior classes, unaccustomed to the exercise of their own free will, dared not to act without the commands of their governments or of their liege lords. These governments became, by the very act of conquest, subordinate to the conquerors; and the liege lords, long accustomed to witness the hourly vexations which the people experienced from the soldiery, resigned themselves the more easily to the evils which war brings in her train.

The clergy in Prussia had but little ascendancy over the people; the reformation has destroyed, among the protestants, that power which the priests preserve, even in our days, in some catholic countries; and especially in Spain. The men of letters, who might have influenced public opinion and made their wisdom subservient to the cause of their country, were but rarely called to take an active part in public affairs. Literary reputation was the only end of their ambition, and they rarely addicted themselves to occupations or studies applicable to existing circumstances. The real power of several states in Germany rested on their military systems, and their political existence could not but depend entirely on the strength or weakness of their governments.

In the plains of Germany the local circumstances of the country did not permit the people to escape so easily from the yoke of their conquerors as in some other countries of a different nature. Small bodies of troops kept a great extent of conquered country in awe, and assured our armies of subsistence. The citizens could have found no secure retreats if they had tried partial revolts against us; besides, the Germans accustomed to a quiet and regular life, are only roused to make a desperate effort by the complete breaking up of all their ordinary habits.

We had nothing to fear from the inhabitants of the countries conquered by our arms, and the war of Germany had been carried on solely by armies of regulars, between

20

whom there exists rather rivalry than hatred. The success of a campaign depended on the aggregate of the military operations, on the activity and perseverance of the commanders, and their skill in discovering and preventing the plans of each other, and in bringing with skill and celerity great masses down on the points of attack. All those little partial actions were avoided, which in war only increase the miseries of individuals without contributing to any important advantage; and the talents of the generals were never baffled by the exertions of individuals, or by the spontaneous movements of the people.

In Germany we had only had to subdue governments and armies; in the Spanish peninsula, where we were now to make war, the government and the army were already annihilated. The Emperor Napoleon had invaded Portugal and Spain, put to flight or reduced to captivity the sovereigns of those two countries and dispersed their military forces. We were not called to fight against troops of the line, everywhere nearly the same, but against a people insulated from all the other continental nations, by its manners, its prejudices, and even the nature of its country. The Spaniards were to oppose to us a resistance so much the more obstinate, as they believed it to be the object of the French government to make the peninsula a secondary state, irrevocably subject to the dominion of France.

With regard to knowledge and the progress of social habits, Spain was at least a century behind the other nations of the continent. The distant and almost insular situation of the country, and the severity of its religious institutions, had prevented the Spaniards from taking part in the disputes and controversies which had agitated and enlightened Europe during the sixteenth century. They scarcely thought more in the eighteenth of the philosophical spirit which had been one of the causes of the revolution in France.

Although the Spaniards were too much given to indolence,

and that there were found in their administration that disorder and corruption which are inevitable consequences of a long despotism, their national character had not been sullied. Their government, arbitrary as it was, bore no resemblance to the absolute military power existing in Germany, where the constant submission of each and every one to the orders of a single one, continually pressed down the springs of individual character. Ferdinand the Catholic, Charles V and Philip II had, it is true, usurped almost all the privileges of the grandees and of the Cortes, and they had annihilated Spanish liberty; but the weakness of government, under their successors, had always left to the people, notwithstanding the despotism of the sovereign, a practical freedom which was often carried even to insubordination.

In the annals of the German monarchies, no names were ever heard but those of the sovereign and his armies. Since Ferdinand the Catholic had united the different kingdoms of Spain, scarcely a single reign had passed in which the people had not given sensible proofs of its existence and power by imposing conditions on its masters, or by expelling their ministers or their favourites.

When the inhabitants of Madrid revolted, and demanded from Charles III, the father of Charles IV, the dismissal of his minister Squilaci, the king himself was obliged to appear in order to compound with the people, and to employ the invention of a monk bearing a crucifix in his hand. The court, which had fled to Aranjuez, attempted afterwards to send the Walloon guards against Madrid: the people killed several, and the cry was, *'Si los Vallones entraran, los Borbones no reinaran'* – 'If the Walloons enter, the Bourbons shall not reign.' The Walloons did not enter, Squilaci was dismissed, and order was restored. At Berlin and in Prussia the inhabitants respected the soldiers of their king, as the soldiers

22

themselves respected their military commanders; at Madrid, the sentinels placed on guard to attend to the execution of the orders of their sovereign yielded the precedence to the meanest burgess.

The revenues of the crown were very scanty, and consequently could maintain but a very limited number of troops. The regiments of the line, with the exception of some privileged corps, were incomplete, ill-paid, and ill-disciplined. The priests were the only powerful executive militia that the kings of Spain could command; it was by the exhortations of the ministers from their altars, and the presentation of pontifical ornaments and relics that they repressed and dissipated popular tumults.

The Spanish priests hated the French from patriotism and from interest; for they well knew that the intention was to abolish their privileges, and to deprive them of their riches and temporal power. Their opinion swayed that of the greatest part of the nation. Every Spaniard regarded the public cause as his own private quarrel, and we had, in short, almost as many individual enemies to fight as the Spanish peninsula contained inhabitants.

The high and barren mountains which surround and intersect Spain were peopled by warlike tribes, always armed for the purpose of smuggling and accustomed to baffle the regular troops of their own country, which were frequently sent in pursuit of them. The untamed character of the inhabitants of the peninsula, the mildness of the climate, which admits of living in the open air almost all the year, and thus to abandon one's dwelling upon occasion; the inaccessible retreats of the inland mountains; the sea, which washes such extensive shores; all the great circumstances arising from the national character, the climate, and local situation, could not fail of procuring for the Spaniards numberless facilities for escaping from the oppression of their conquerors, and for multiplying their own forces,

23

whether by transporting them rapidly to those points on which the French were weak, or in securing their escape from pursuit.

When we quitted our cantonments in Prussia to go to Spain, towards the end of August 1808, we had scarcely reflected on the unforeseen obstacles which we might encounter in a country so new to us. We fancied we were marching on a short and easy expedition: conquerors in Germany, we did not imagine that anything was to stop us in future.

Our soldiers never inquired what country we were leading them to: but if there were provisions where they were going, it was the only point of view in which they ever considered the geography of the earth. The world was divided by them into two parts, the happy zone, in which the vine grows, and the detestable zone, which is without it.

Having heard at the beginning of every campaign that they were called upon to strike the last blow at the tottering power of the English, they confounded this power in all its forms with England itself. They judged of the distance which separated them from it by the number of marches they had made for so many years from one end of the world to the other, without having yet reached this kind of imaginary and distant country which was constantly receding from them. At length, said they, if the desert separated us from it in Egypt, and the sea at Boulogne, we shall reach it by land after we have crossed Spain.

After having passed the Elbe and the Weser, we reached the left bank of the Rhine and France. For two months an approaching war with Austria had been talked of, and when we quitted Prussia in the month of September 1808, we were persuaded that we were to be sent to the Danube. It was with deep sorrow and almost with tears in their eyes that our hussars quitted Germany, that beautiful country that

24

they had then conquered, that land of war from which they bore so many remembrances of glory, and where they had even sometimes made themselves individually beloved.

We traversed France as if it had been a land newly conquered and subjected to our arms. The Emperor Napoleon had ordered that his soldiers should be well received and feasted everywhere; deputations came to compliment us at the gates of his good cities. The officers and soldiers were conducted immediately on their arrival to sumptuous banquets prepared beforehand, and on our departure, the magistrates thanked us again that we had deigned to spend in one day many weeks' private revenues of their municipal chests. The soldiers of the grand army did not lose in France the habit they had contracted in Germany, of now and then maltreating the citizens or peasants with whom they lodged. The allied auxiliaries, in particular, would not comprehend why they were not to behave in France as in an enemy's country; they said it must be the custom, as the French troops had not behaved otherwise to them in Germany and in Poland.

The inhabitants of the towns and villages through which we passed, suffered all patiently till the armed torrent was drained off. Our troops were composed, besides the French, of Germans, Italians, Poles, Swiss, Dutch, and even Irish and Mameluks; these strangers were all dressed in their national uniforms, and spoke their own languages; but notwithstanding the dissimilarity of manners which raise barriers between nations, military discipline easily united them all under the powerful hand of one; all these men wore the same cockade, and they had but one shout of war, and one cry to rally.

We crossed the Seine at Paris, the Loire at Saumur, the Garonne at Bordeaux; there, for the first time since we left Prussia, we enjoyed a few days of rest, while the rest of the army was employed in gaining the other bank of the river.

We next traversed the uncultivated tract between Bordeaux and Bayonne. In these solitary plains, as in the moors of Prussia and Poland, the sandy soil no longer resounded under the horses' feet, the regular and accelerated noise of their iron-shod hoofs no longer served to renew their ardour. Vast forests of pine and of cork bound the horizon at an immense distance; one sees at long intervals single shepherds, clad in black sheep-skins, mounted on stilts six or seven feet high, and leaning on a long pole; they remain motionless on the same spot, without ever losing sight of their flocks which feed around them on the heath.

When the Emperor Napoleon crossed these wide plains, the poverty of the country did not permit it to furnish the usual horse guard of honour: he was escorted by a detachment of these shepherds, who, with their tall stilts, kept pace through the sand with the horses at full trot.

Some leagues beyond Bayonne we reached the Bidassoa, a rivulet which bounds France in the Pyrenees. As soon as one sets one's foot on the Spanish territory, one perceives a sensible difference in the aspect of the country, and in the manners of the inhabitants. The narrow crooked streets of the towns, the grated windows, the doors of the houses always carefully shut, the severe and reserved air of the inhabitants of all classes, the distrust which was generally shown towards us, increased the involuntary melancholy which seized us on our entrance into Spain.

We saw the Emperor Napoleon pass before he arrived at Vittoria; he was on horseback; the simplicity of his green uniform distinguished him amidst the richly clothed generals who surrounded him; he waved his hands to every individual officer as he passed, seeming to say, 'I rely on you.' The French and the Spaniards were gathered in crowds on his way: the first regarded him as the fortune of the whole army; the Spaniards seemed willing to read in his aspect and behaviour the fate of their unhappy country.

During the last days of October 1808, the French army in Spain, commanded by King Joseph, was successively joined by the grand army of Germany. It was only then that we learned with astonishment from our brethren in arms, a part of the events of the Peninsular war, and the details of the unfortunate affairs which had forced the Generals Dupont and Junot to capitulate in Andalusia and in Portugal, Marshal Moncey to retire from before Valentia, and, in short, the whole army to concentrate itself on the left bank of the Ebro.*

*King Joseph was at Vittoria with the general staff and his guards. Marshal Moncey, with his *corps d'armée*, was at Tafalla, observing and watching the Spanish army of General Palafox, placed at Sanguessa, on the frontiers of Navarre and Arragon. The troops under Marshal Ney occupied Logrono and Guardia; they had before them, in the neighbourhood of Tudela, on the Ebro, the Spanish armies commanded by the Generals Castanos and Palafox, who, when united, might be about 40,000 strong. Marshal Bessières was at Miranda, on the Ebro: on retiring, he had left a garrison in the fort of Pancorvo; his position was covered by the numerous and well-mounted calvary of General Lassalle. Marshal Lefevre occupied Durango: the corps commanded by the Marshals Bessières and Lefevre were opposed to the centre and the left wing of the Spaniards, under Generals Belvedere and Blake. The Spanish army of the centre, placed at Burgos, was only from 12 to 14,000 strong. It was to be reinforced by 26,000 English, who were advancing from Portugal and Corunna, under Generals Moore and Sir D. Baird. This force was intended to sustain the army of the right, commanded by General Blake, in Biscay, and to keep up the communication with the Spanish armies in Arragon and Navarre.

The army of General Blake, although 30,000 strong, had but little cavalry, therefore it dared not come down into the plains in the neighbourhood of Miranda and Vittoria: it had quitted its positions between Ona Frias and Erron to seize Bilbao, and it had advanced through the mountains which separate Biscay from the province of Alava, as far as Zornosa and Archandiano, towards Durango, to raise the country and to attack the right, and cut off the communications of the army of King Joseph. The Spanish armies of Navarre and Arragon were to make the

27

The 8th of November, in the night, the imperial quarters were removed from Vittoria to Miranda. The next day the whole of the centre, of which we were a part, marched under the immediate orders of the Emperor. We were to make a powerful attack on Burgos, where the centre of the Spanish forces were placed, then to threaten, by advancing rapidly, the flanks of their armies of the right and left in Biscay and towards the frontiers of Navarre and Arragon; to prevent those armies from concentrating themselves towards Madrid, if they retired; and to cut off, by throwing ourselves on their rear, all their communications if they attempted resistance.

To effect this, our army of the right, formed of the corps of Marshals Victor and Lefevre, were to continue marching against the army of Blake, who was retiring upon Espinosa after having been repulsed from Durango and Valmaceda. Our army of the left, under Marshals Lannes and Moncey, remained in the neighbourhood of Logrono and Tafalla; it awaited the result of the action that we expected without fail at Burgos, in order to move and go up the Ebro, towards Saragossa.

The imperial headquarters were fixed, on the night of the 9th, at Briviesca; the army under the orders of the Emperor was cantoned in the neighbourhood of that town. The

---

same movement against the centre and the left of the French, in order to force them to retire by the road of Tolosa, or drive them into the defiles of Navarre, towards Pampeluna. Such were the projects of the Spaniards, and the situation of affairs, when the Emperor Napoleon took the command of the armies in Spain.

The 31st of October, the corps of Marshal Lefevre had attacked the army of General Blake, near Durango; he had repulsed him, and entered Bilbao the next day. The corps of Marshal Victor moved, on the 6th November, from Vittoria to Ordunna; it was to form, with that of Marshal Lefevre, the right of our army.

inhabitants of the country had everywhere fled to the mountains on our approach.

At daybreak on the 10th, Marshal Soult went, with a division of infantry, to reconoitre the positions of the enemy in the direction of Burgos. On his arrival at the village of Gamonal, he was received by a discharge of thirty pieces of cannon – this was to the French the signal for attack. Marshal Soult did not wait for the rest of the army which was following him; he engaged immediately, and overthrew the Walloons and Spanish guards, which formed the chief strength of the enemy. Marshal Bessières, arriving soon after with the cavalry, turned the enemy's wings, completed the rout, and entered Burgos pel-mel with the fugitives.

Of all the army, our brigade of hussars had remained alone in an obscure cantonment, two leagues in the rear of Briviesca. The adjutant who was to have brought us our orders to march lost his way, not being able to procure a guide, and we only began our march at nine o'clock in the morning. We followed the track of the army all day, without even surmising what had passed in the morning in our front.

When night came, we perceived, at a great distance, the fires of the vanguard of the army. Notwithstanding the darkness, we discovered, by the motions of our horses, that we were crossing a field of battle; they slackened their pace every moment, raising their feet cautiously, for fear of touching the dead over whom they were passing. They stopped sometimes to put down their heads, and smelt with horror to the carcasses of the horses killed during the action.

Burgos had been entirely abandoned by its inhabitants. That great city was only a vast solitude when our troops arrived there immediately after the battle, and it was given up to be plundered. In the quarter by which we entered were heard on all sides the hum and confused voices of the soldiers, who were going and coming in all directions in search of provisions and utensils through the deserted houses. To light themselves they carried enormous torches, which they had found in the neighbouring convents. A little farther, in a part of the city less visited by the troops, were heard doleful and stifled groans from the aged and the sick, who, unable to fly, had taken refuge in a church, where they were crowded together in great numbers. They were repeating prayers with their clergy, expecting a death which they believed to be near; the feeble rays of the sacred lamp shot through the lattices of the church. We passed between two high walls of enormous bales of wools, which the Spaniards had collected from all quarters, to carry with the baggage of their army into the south of France, so certain did they think themselves of gaining a great victory over us.

At eleven o'clock at night we arrived at the bivouac designed for us, near the banks of the Arlanzon. When the day came, we saw in the low river which ran by us the bodies of a few Spanish soldiers and monks, who had died in battle the day before.

At sunrise on the 11th, our brigade of light cavalry set off to explore the country up the Arlanzon. We discovered at a distance, on the banks of the river, troops of peasants and of the inhabitants of the town retiring behind the heights, or among the precipices of the opposite shore. Frequently we perceived nothing but their heads, raised from time to time above the brushwood to see if we had passed.

Some of our flank companies met some nuns, who had quitted Burgos during the battle the day before. These poor creatures, some of whom had never been without the precincts of their cloister, had walked in their fright as far as their limbs could bear them without stopping, and had tried to conceal themselves in the groves near the river.

On first seeing us at a distance they had dispersed, but on our nearer approach they gathered together, and remained on their knees, close to each other, with their heads hanging down and enveloped in their hoods. She who had preserved most presence of mind, placed herself upright before her companions. On her face was an air of candour and dignity, and that kind of calmness which is given by strong emotions in a moment of despair. The nun who stood up said, as she touched the beads of her rosary, to the soldiers who passed nearest, as if to implore their protection, the only three words she knew of our language, 'Bonjour, Messieurs François.' These poor nuns were left in peace.

We spent four days in a town about four leagues from Burgos, of whose name I am ignorant, because we found no person to inquire it of. The imperial quarters remained at Burgos till the 22nd.

This town was the centre of all the military operations, and from thence it was equally easy to communicate with the armies of Biscay and Arragon, to observe their marches and to assist them in case of need.

The day after the affair of Burgos, numerous detachments were sent in all directions in pursuit of the enemy, in order to complete the destruction of an army which an easy victory had dispersed, but which still might not be wholly annihilated. Ten thousand cavalry, with twenty pieces of light artillery, set off to fall rapidly, by way of Placentia, Leon, and Zamora, on the rear of the English army, which was believed to be at Valladolid. Marshal Soult threw himself, by Villarcayo and Reynosa, behind the Spanish army of the left. A division of infantry went by a more direct route to occupy the defiles of the mountains towards St Ander; these troops, notwithstanding the rapidity of their march, did not come up with the enemy.

The army of General Blake, in retreat ever since the affair of Durango, had vainly tried to rally at Guenes and at Valmaceda successively. Pursued by Marshal Victor in the direction of Espinosa, and by Marshal Lefevre in that of

Villarcayo, it had at length been totally defeated, on the 10th of November, at Espinosa, after two days' fighting.

The Spanish armies of the centre and of the left having been beaten at all points, there only remained the army of the right to disperse before we should march to Madrid. To this end the army of Marshal Ney was sent from Burgos, by Lerma and Aranda, up the Douro, and down again towards the Ebro, in order to turn the corps of Generals Castanos and Palafox, who were shortly to be attacked in front by our army of the left, under the orders of Marshals Lannes and Moncey. These French corps of the left still occupied Logrono and Tafalla, and were preparing to go down the Ebro.

On the 15th of November, our brigade of hussars went to Lerma, to join the corps of Marshal Ney, to which it thenceforth remained provisionally attached. On the 16th, Marshal Ney's corps went from Lerma to Aranda: the inhabitants always abandoned their dwellings at our approach, carrying with them into their mountain retreats all their most precious possessions. The solitude and the desolation, which victorious armies commonly leave behind them, seemed to precede us wherever we came.

In approaching the deserted towns and villages of Castile, we no longer saw those clouds of smoke, which, constantly rising through the air, form a second atmosphere over inhabited and populous cities. Instead of living sounds and continual rumours, we heard nothing within the circles of their walls but the passing bells, which our arrival could not suspend, or the croaking of the ravens hovering round the high belfries. The houses, now empty, served only to re-echo tardily and discordantly the deep sounds of the drum, or the shrills notes of the trumpet.

Lodgings were quickly distributed; every regiment occupied a ward, every company a street, according to the size of the town. A very short time after our entry, the soldiers were established in their new dwellings, as if they had come to found a colony. This warlike and transitory population gave new names to the places it occupied – they talked of the 'Dragoon-ward', such a company's street'; 'Our general's house'; 'the main-guard square', or 'Parade-place.' Often on the walls of a convent might be read, written with charcoal, 'Barracks of such a battalion.' From the cell of a deserted cloister, hung a sign with a French inscription, bearing the name of one of the first cooks in Paris; he was a victualler, who had hastened to set up his ambulatory tavern in that spot.

When the army arrived late at night in the place where it was to rest, it was impossible to distribute the quarters with regularity, and we lodged *militarily*, that is to say, promiscuously and without observing any order, wherever we could find room. As soon as the main guard was posted, at a concerted signal the soldiers left the ranks, and precipitated themselves all together tumultuously, like a torrent, through the city, and long after the arrival of the army shrieks were still heard, and the noise of doors broken open with hatchets or great stones. Some of the grenadiers found out a method, as quick as efficacious, to force such doors as obstinately resisted; they fired point blank into the key-holes of the locks, and thus rendered vain the precautions of the inhabitants, who always carefully locked up in their houses before they fled, at our approach, to the mountains.

On the morning of the 20th, Marshal Ney's corps left Aranda. For two days we continued to march up the banks of the Douro, having no news of the enemy, and not meeting any where a living creature. On the 21st, a little before sunset, we suddenly remarked a little vacillation in the movements of our advanced skirmishers; we immediately formed in squadrons, and shortly afterwards a detachment of our advanced guard was engaged with a corps of the enemy, which it easily repulsed; we made some prisoners as we entered Almazan.

Marshal Ney's corps bivouacked under the walls of that town for the night; the inhabitants had entirely deserted it. It was too late to make regular distributions, and, unfortunately, we could not prevent plunder during half an hour, to satisfy the immediate necessities of the troops. We sent, that same night, several parties of twenty-five hussars each, to reconnoitre in different directions. The detachment which had pursued the road to Siguenza came back during the night, with some baggage and a few prisoners.

The next day, being the 22nd November, Marshal Ney's army set out for Soria. The 2nd Hussars, our regiment, was left alone at Almazan, to guard the communication with Burgos by Aranda, and to watch the enemy's corps, which were said to be in the neighbourhood of Siguenza, Medina Cœli, and Agreda.

I received, at daybreak on the 24th, orders to go with twenty-five horse and reconnoitre on the direct road from Almazan to Agreda. Not being able to procure a guide I went with my detachment up the right bank of the Douro in the direction indicated by a bad French map, which led me into an error and we lost our way. We perceived, after four hours' painful march, through crossroads, two children who fled towards the thicket, screaming with terror. I followed them, and suddenly found myself alone in an encampment of women, who had fled from their village with their sheep and their children, and had taken refuge in a little island in the river.

I arrived so completely unawares that I had time to assure them of safety before my detachment could follow me. I made my interpreter, who was with me, ask them which was the direct road from Almazan to Agreda. An aged pastor, the only man who was with the women, answered that I had wandered from it above four leagues, and he pointed out the right road on the other side of the river. We passed through a line of villages and little towns where the only inhabitants were men, and we at length arrived at our place of destination.

The interpreter whom I made use of, was a Flemish deserter, whom hunger, and the fear of being murdered by the peasants of the country, had forced to come to us after the affair of Burgos. We had nicknamed him Blanco, because, to keep himself warm, he had covered his old Walloon uniform, which was worn out and torn, with a white Dominican habit which the hussars had given him, and he also wore on his head the enormous hat of that religious order. In the inhabited villages we went through the peasants fancied, when they saw him on foot marching at our head, that he was really a monk whom we had forced to accompany us; they saluted him profoundly, pitied his unhappy fate, and all gave money to the reverend father, who, proud of so many honours, would not, even when he had an opportunity, quit his lucrative costume.

For want of being able to procure a guide before we left Almazan, we lost our way, and were nine hours marching only four miles. The difficulty of getting guides was continually recurring because the inhabitants deserted their villages on our approach.

Our regiment received orders to quit Almazan the same night. We marched nearly a night and a day without stopping, and joined Marshal Ney just as he was entering Agreda by the road from Soria. The infantry lodged in the town. The light cavalry was sent a league farther, on the road to Cascante, in order to cover the position of the army. We believed ourselves to be close upon the rear of the left wing of the Spanish forces.

The city of Agreda was deserted: the staff officer of our brigade of hussars in vain endeavoured to find a guide in it,

35

and we were obliged to go, according to our map only, in search of the cantonment designed for us. Night overtook us, we soon lost ourselves in the mountains; misled by the deceptions of a misty darkness we always fancied ourselves on the brink of some precipice. Whenever we had marched a hundred paces we made a long halt, while those who were at the head of the column almost groped their way between the rocks, and we long heard in the deep silence of the night the uncertain tread of feet, and the shudderings of the horses who were gnawing the bit, impatient to get on to rest.

We had alighted and were marching in file, listening to, and repeating by turns, the warnings of holes or of precipices, which were given in an under voice, in order not to awake a corps whose half-extinguished fires we saw on the opposite side of a deep ravine. We knew not whether they were friends or foes, and in our situation an attack of infantry must have been fatal to us.

We thus passed the greater part of the night in marching and counter-marching. The moon rose a little before daybreak; we found ourselves nearly in the place from which we had set out the night before, and we at length saw, at the bottom of a narrow valley, the village where we should have passed the night: we had been marching above thirty hours. The impossibility of finding guides thus offered to us at every step a thousand difficulties in detail, of an entire new kind. In these scantily peopled countries, where the whole population was against us, we rarely found individuals who, even for the purpose of misleading, were capable of giving us the slightest information concerning the enemy.

We learned, but too late, that the armies of Generals Castanos and Palafox had been completely defeated, at Tudela, on the 23rd; if we had arrived a day sooner at Agreda, we should have met and taken in that town the dispersed columns of Spaniards, who were retiring upon Madrid.

II

THE LEFT of our army, whose movements we were to second, had concentrated itself on the 22nd, at the bridge of Lodosa. On the 23rd, it met the Spanish right, drawn up in battle array, of a league in extent, between the town of Tudela and the village of Cascante. Marshal Lannes broke the centre of the enemy's line, by a division of infantry marched in close column; General Lefevre's cavalry immediately passed through the opening, and, by an oblique movement, surrounded the Spanish right. Once broken on any point, they could no longer manœuvre, and they retired in disorder, leaving thirty pieces of cannon, many dead, and a great number of prisoners on the field.

Since the retreat of King Joseph on the Ebro in July, the Spaniards had acquired so great a confidence in their own strength, that their anxiety, when they were to come to action with us, was not so much concerning the means of resisting us, or of securing their retreat in case of a reverse, as lest a Frenchman should escape them.

They prejudged the event of the battle, by their own ardent desire to conquer and destroy their enemies. Ignorant of the art of manœuvring, being afraid of not spreading their columns in time to surround us, they placed

37

themselves in long shallow lines, in plains where the superiority of our tactics, and of our cavalry, must necessarily give us the advantage. This order of battle, bad even for well manœuvred troops, deprived the Spaniards of the power of reinforcing the points attacked by our close columns fast enough, or of concentrating themselves to resist our masses. Our troops had met with more resistance in Biscay and the Asturias, because they had had to fight in mountainous countries, where the difficulties of the ground, and the courage of individuals, may sometimes baffle the calculations of military art. Before they could reach Reinosa, they had been obliged to conquer at Durango, at Zornosa, at Guenes, at Valmaceda, and last at Espinosa.

Not a Frenchman then doubted that such rapid victories must have decided the fate of the Spaniards. We believed, and Europe believed it too, that we had only to march to Madrid to complete the subjection of Spain, and to organise the country in the French manner, that is to say, to increase our means of conquest by all the resources of our vanquished enemies. The wars we had hitherto carried on had accustomed us to see in a nation only its military forces, and to count for nothing the spirit which might animate its citizens.

On the 26th November, Marshal Ney's corps moved, by Cascante, upon Borja. A division of General Maurice Mathieu preceded us by a day, making a number of prisoners on its march. The 27th we arrived at Alagon, a little town situated four leagues from Saragossa, whose numerous steeples appeared in the distance.

The Arragonese had not allowed themselves to be cast down by the recent reverses of their armies; they had resolved to defend themselves in Saragossa. They had not been able to surround themselves by regular fortifications, but they had converted every dwelling into a separate fortress, and every convent, every house, required a separate assault. This kind of fortification is, perhaps, the best of all calculated to lengthen out a siege.

Palafox had just thrown himself into the town with 10,000 men, whom he had saved after the battle of Tudela, and these same soldiers of the army of Arragon, that we had defeated almost without an effort in the flat country, as citizens within the walls of their capital town, resisted us nearly twelve months.

Fifty thousand peasants, in arms, collected to defend Saragossa: they threw themselves from every side into the town, even through the midst of our victorious troops, dreading lest they should arrive too late where their hearts and their country called them. The miraculous virgin of Pilar, said they, has protected us for ages; in happy times we crowded as pilgrims to her shrine, to obtain abundant harvests, and now we will not leave her altars defenceless.

The character of the Spaniards in these provinces has no resemblance to that of other European nations. Their patriotism is a religion, as it was with the ancients, among whom no nation allowed itself to despair, or owned itself conquered even in the midst of disasters. The sacred eagles of the god of the Capitol, borne aloft in battle, led the Romans on to victory; and when, subsequent to the times of chivalry, our modern armies were organized in the Roman forms, the point of honour took place in our regular troops of that religious sentiment, which attached the Roman soldier to his standard. Discipline, founded on the military point of honour, has taught modern armies to triumph; but it is patriotism alone, political or religious, which can render nations invincible.

The people of Spain in general were animated solely by religious patriotism; they had no practical knowledge of discipline, or of the laws of war. They easily abandoned their standards after a reverse of fortune; they never considered themselves bound to keep faith with their enemies,

39

but they had but one interest, but one sentiment – to revenge, by every possible means, the wrongs that the French had done their country.

One of the insurgent peasants of Arragon, among others, was seized by our skirmishers; he was only armed with a gun, and was driving before him an ass, laden with some months' provisions. The officer who commanded the advanced guard took pity on him, and ordered him to be set at liberty, making signs to him to escape. The peasant at once appeared to comprehend; but, left to himself, he loaded his gun, and came back immediately to our ranks to fire at his deliverer. Happily the ball missed. This peasant hoped to die a martyr, for killing one whom he had mistaken for one of our principal chiefs. On halting, he was brought before the colonel of the regiment.

We surrounded him from curiosity. A motion of one of our hussars persuaded him that he was going to be shot; he immediately, and proudly, knelt down, prayed to God and the Virgin Mary, and thus awaited his death. We raised him, and at night he was sent to headquarters. If these men had known how to fight as well as how to die, we should not so easily have passed the Pyrenees.

The division of Marshal Lannes remained in Arragon to besiege Saragossa; that of Marshal Ney continued by forced marches to pursue the remains of the army of Castanos, which was retiring on Guadalaxara and Madrid. The 28th, the advanced division cut to pieces the Spanish rearguard, which attempted to defend the defile of Buvierca on the Xalon.

The forced marches of our army often continued till late at night, and in passing the squadrons we frequently heard Italians, Germans or Frenchmen, singing their national airs to lull their fatigue, or, in this distant and hostile land, to recall a lively remembrance of their absent country.

The army stopped very late at night near deserted towns

or villages, and on our arrival, we generally found ourselves in absolute want of everything; but the soldiers soon dispersed on all sides to forage, and in less than an hour they collected, at the bivouac, all that yet remained in the neighbouring villages.

Around large fires, lighted at intervals, all the implements of military cookery were seen. Here they were busy constructing in haste, barracks of plank covered with leaves for want of straw; there they were erecting tents, by stretching across four stakes such pieces of stuff' as had been found in the deserted houses. The ground was strewed up and down with the skins of the sheep just slain, guitars, pitchers, bladders of wine, the cowls of monks, clothes of every form and colour; here the calvary under arms were sleeping by the side of their horses, farther on a few of the infantry, dressed in women's clothes, were dancing grotesquely among piles of arms to the sound of discordant music.

The moment the army departed, the peasants descended from the neighbouring heights and started up on every hand, as if out of the bosom of the earth, from their hiding-places. They hastened back to their dwellings. Our soldiers could neither go off the roads nor lag behind the columns, without exposing themselves to being assassinated by the peasants of the mountains, and we dared not, as in Germany, place detached patrols or send our sick by themselves to the hospitals. The foot soldiers, who could no longer bear the march, followed their divisions on asses; they held their long muskets in their left hands, and in their right their bayonets, which they used as goads. These pacific animals, like the untamed Numidian steeds of former times, had neither bridles nor saddles.

On the 1st December we were to sleep in a village situated a league to the north of Guadalaxara; the billets were distributed, we were going to break our ranks and to disperse into quarters, when some one came to inform us that they saw at a distance some of the enemy's soldiers flying. It appeared difficult to reach them, and two or three of the youngest of us undertook, as sport, to pursue them; after having received a sign of approbation from the colonel. I fixed on one in particular, who ran faster than the others. He had on a uniform of azure blue, tolerably bright, which, at a distance, led me at first to take him for an officer.

When he saw that he could not escape, he stopped and waited for me on the opposite side of a ditch he had just lightly leaped. I thought at first that he was going to level his piece at me, but when I came within twenty paces of him he let fall his arms, took off his hat, and said several times over, making the most profound bows in all the positions: 'Monsieur, j'ai l'honneur de vous saluer; Monsieur, je suis votre très humble serviteur.'

I stopped, as much astonished at his grotesque figure as at hearing him speak French. I relieved him, assuring him he had nothing to fear. He told me that he was a dancing-master, a native of Thoulouse; that at the time of the rising en masse in Andalusia, he had been put in the pillory for a fortnight, in order to force him to serve in the regiment of Ferdinand VII, the uniform of which he then wore; which, as he said, was most contrary to his pacific genius. I told him to go to the village where the regiment was. We also made another Frenchman prisoner, he was the son of one of the first magistrates of the town of Pau in Béarn.*

Hurried on by the pleasure of the ride and the impetuosity of my horse, I climbed one hill, which lay before me, then another. I crossed a torrent, and arrived, after

*The second of these Frenchmen alone joined the regiment; a few days afterwards the means of escape were given him. They were afraid of sending him to the depot of prisoners, lest he should be shot for having been taken under arms, and in a Spanish uniform.

half an hour's hard riding, at the entrance of a large village, which I went into. The inhabitants, having seen me coming from afar, were afraid that I should be followed by a numerous body. The alarm instantly spread among them, and they hurried from all quarters to their houses, where they were occupied in barricading the street-doors, preparing, according to their custom, to escape over the walls of the back courts.

Seeing that I was alone, they gradually came out of their dwellings to the market-place, where I had stopped. I heard several men repeat, with considerable energy, the word *matar*; as I did not then know the Spanish language, I thought at first that it was a manner of expressing their astonishment at the sight of a stranger. I afterwards learnt that the word means *to kill*.

The Spaniards were not so peaceable as the inhabitants of the plains of Germany, where a single French soldier gives laws to a whole town. When I saw the crowd increase, and the agitation augment, I began to fear lest the inhabitants should detain me as a prisoner, and deliver me to the enemy. I spurred my horse on both sides, and went without the village, placing myself on a hillock, where I was soon followed both by the men and the women; I then began to make my horse curvet, and made him leap backwards and forwards over a low wall and a ditch behind me, to shew the inhabitants that I was not afraid of them, and I could easily escape when I pleased.

Detained by curiosity (it was the first time since we passed the Ebro that I had seen a village entirely inhabited, and above all by women,) I returned to the height where I had at first placed myself, and made a sign with my scabbard to the people, who began anew to approach me, not to come within ten paces, and tried to make them understand that my horse wanted food.

The inhabitants, wrapped up in their great cloaks,

looked at me in silence, with a kind of astonishment, keeping up, nevertheless, in their looks and behaviour, that gravity and that dignity which characterize the Castilians of every age and of every class. They appeared heartily to despise a stranger, ignorant of their language.

When I saw that they would not comprehend me, I tried a few words of Latin. That language was often useful to us in Spain, to make ourselves understood by the clergy, who generally speak it tolerably well. A young student stepped out of the crowd, and came back a few moments afterwards with the village schoolmaster; he was so pleased to speak Latin, and to tell me how he had acquired such a degree of knowledge, that he procured for me all I wanted, and I set off soon afterwards. When our regiment passed through this same village, the next morning, it was completely deserted. I lost my way in the dark as I went back to my quarters, and only joined my comrades at midnight.

The next day, 2nd December, we took up our quarters in the neighbourhood of the town of Alcala de Henares. We met a squadron of Polish lancers, which Marshal Bessières had sent from St Augustin to reconnoitre towards Guadalaxara; from them we learned, that the advanced guard of the army of the centre had arrived before Madrid. We were now only three leagues from that capital.

The Emperor Napoleon had set out on the 22nd November, from Burgos, for Aranda, in order to observe, and support, if necessary, the movements of the army of the left, upon the Ebro, against the Spanish right. The 20th November, nine days after the affair of Tudela, the Emperor had marched against Madrid, with the army of the centre, by the direct road of the Castiles: he had left Marshal Soult's corps towards Asturia, to watch the remains of the Spanish army of Galicia.

The vanguard of the Emperor's army arrived, at daybreak,

on the 30th, at the foot of the mountain called Somo Sierra. The *Puerto*, a passage of this mountain, was defended by a division of from 12 to 15,000 Spaniards, and by a battery of sixteen pieces of cannon. Three regiments of infantry, of the first division, and six pieces of cannon, commenced the attack. The Polish lancers of the guard then charged along the causeway, and carried the enemy's batteries by assault. The Spaniards, too weak to resist the Emperor Napoleon's army, sought safety on every side, by flying to the rocks.

The imperial headquarters were fixed, on the 1st December, at St Augustino. Marshal Ney's corps, to which our regiment was attached, arrived the same day, by Guadalaxara and Alcala, to join the Emperor.

On the 2nd December, in the morning, the Emperor Napoleon preceded the main body of his army, and arrived, with his calvary only, on the heights, close to the capital of Spain. Instead of the order one commonly perceives on approaching fortified towns, where all the circumstances of war are foreseen, instead of that silence, which is only interrupted by the deep and lengthened call of 'Sentry, take heed!' by which the sentinels, placed round a rampart, make sure of each other's vigilance, were heard the bells of the 600 churches of Madrid, ringing in continued peals, and, from time to time, the sharp cries of the mob, and the quick roll of the drum.

The inhabitants of Madrid had only thought of their defence eight days before the arrival of the French armies, and all their preparations were marked by precipitation and inexperience. They had placed artillery behind sandbags and barricades, or raised entrenchments, in haste, with bales of wool or cotton. The houses, at the entrance of the principal streets, were filled with armed men, placed behind mattresses, at the windows. The Retiro alone had been fortified with any care; it is a royal castle, situated on a height which commands the capital.

One of Marshal Bessières' aides-de-camp was sent, according to the custom, in the morning, to summon Madrid. He narrowly escaped being torn to pieces by the inhabitants, when he proposed their submitting to the French: he owed his life to the protection of the Spanish troops of the line.

The Emperor Napoleon employed the evening in reconnoitring the environs of the city, and in fixing his plan of attack. The first columns of the infantry having arrived, at seven o'clock in the evening, a brigade of the first division, supported by four pieces of artillery, marched against the suburbs, and the sharpshooters of the 16th Regiment seized the great burying-ground, after having dislodged the Spaniards from some advanced houses. The night was employed in placing the artillery, in making every preparation for an assault on the following day.

A Spanish officer, taken at Somo Sierra, whom the Prince of Neufchâtel sent at midnight into Madrid, returned some hours afterwards to say that the inhabitants persisted in defending themselves; and, on the 3rd, at nine o'clock in the morning, the cannonade began.

Thirty pieces of cannon, under the command of General Cenarmont, battered the walls of the Retiro, while twenty pieces of artillery of the guard, and some light troops, made a false attack in another quarter, to distract the attention of the enemy, and to oblige him to divide his forces. The light companies of Villatte's division entered the garden of the Retiro by the breach, and were soon followed by their battalion, and in less than an hour the 4,000 Spanish regulars who defended this important point were overthrown. At eleven o'clock, our soldiers already occupied the important posts of the observatory, the china manufactory, the great barracks, and the palace of Medina Cœli. Masters of all the

Retiro, the French might have burned Madrid in a few hours.

The cannonade then ceased to be heard, the progress of the troops was stopped in every direction, and a third envoy was sent into the place. It was of consequence to the Emperor to conciliate the capital of the kingdom he destined for his brother. One may establish a camp, but not a court, in the midst of ruins. Madrid, in ashes, might by its example have excited a desperate resistance in the other cities of the kingdom. Besides, its destruction would have deprived the French armies of immense resources.

At five o'clock in the afternoon, General Morla, chief of the military junto, and Don B. Yriarte, deputed from the city, came back with the French envoy. They were conducted to the Prince of Neufchâtel's tent. They demanded a suspension of arms during the 4th that they might have time to persuade the people to give themselves up.

The Emperor reproached them with the greatest appearance of anger, for the not executing the treaty of Baylen, and for the massacre of the French prisoners in Andalusia. He wished to frighten the Spanish deputies by this feigned wrath, in order that they might, on their return, communicate their terrors to whose whom they commanded. The Emperor earnestly desired the reduction of Madrid to have appearance of a voluntary submission. It was then generally believed that the whole of Spain would follow the example of the capital.

Meantime the inhabitants refused to lay down their arms, and they continued to fire upon the French, from the windows of the houses surrounding the public walk of the Prado. By the prisoners which were every moment brought in, accounts of the fury and consternation of the city were received. Fifty thousand armed inhabitants, without any discipline, ran up and down the streets tumultuously, vociferating for orders, and accusing their leaders of treason. The Captain General Marquis of Castellar and the other military men of rank left Madrid during the night, with the regular troops, and sixteen pieces of cannon. On the 4th December, at six o'clock in the morning, General Morla and Don F. de Vera came back to the Prince of Neufchâtel's tent, and at ten o'clock the French troops took possession of Madrid.

The Emperor remained with his guard encamped on the heights of Chamartin. According to his usual system of war, he sent numerous bodies in all directions, on the very day of the taking of Madrid to prevent the enemy from having time to reassemble; and to profit by the astonishment and terror which almost always double the forces of the conqueror after any great event, and for the moment paralyse the arms of the conquered.

Marshal Bessières, with sixteen squadrons, pursued the Spanish army of General la Penna, on the road of Valencia. That same army was thrown back upon Cuenca, by General Rufin's division of infantry and General Bordesoult's brigade of dragoons. Marshal Victor's corps went to Toledo, by Aranjuez. Generals Lasalle and Milhaud's divisions of cavalry followed towards Talavera de la Reyna the wreck of the Spanish division, which had been defeated at Somo Sierra, and the troops which had escaped from Madrid. General La Houssaye entered the Escurial.

Our regiment of hussars had passed the 2nd, 3rd, and 4th December in the neighbourhood of Alcala, three leagues from Madrid. On the 5th we received orders to join the imperial headquarters early, in order to be reviewed. We had not been arrived many minutes, on a plain, near the castle of Chamartin, before the Emperor Napoleon suddenly appeared. He was accompanied by the Prince of Neufchâtel, and by five or six aides-de-camp, who could scarcely keep up with him, so hard was he riding.

All the trumpets sounded; the Emperor placed himself about a hundred paces in front of the centre of our regiment, and asked the colonel for the list of officers, non-commissioned officers and privates, who had merited military distinction. The colonel immediately called them by their names. The Emperor Napoleon spoke familiarly to some of the common soldiers who were presented to him; then addressing himself to the general commanding the brigade of which we formed a part, he rapidly put two or three short questions to him; the general having begun to answer rather diffusely, the Emperor Napoleon turned his horse without waiting for the end of the speech, and his departure was as sudden and as swift as his arrival.

After the review we took the road towards Madrid. A melancholy silence had succeeded to the noisy and tumultuous agitation which had reigned only the day before, both within and without the walls of that capital. The streets by which we entered were deserted, and in the public places, even the numerous shops for eatables had not been re-opened. The water carriers were the only inhabitants who had not interrupted their customary employ. They walk along calling, with the slow nasal accent of their native mountains of Galicia, 'Quien quière agua'? Nobody appeared to buy, the *aguador* from time to time ruefully answered himself, '*Dios que la da,*' and began his cry again.

As we advanced towards the centre of Madrid, we saw a few groups of Spaniards standing upright, wrapped in their great cloaks, at the corners of a place where they were formerly used to assemble in great numbers. They looked at us with a melancholy and dejected air; their national pride was so great that they could hardly persuade themselves that soldiers not born Spaniards could have beaten Spaniards. When, by chance, they discovered among our ranks a horse, taken from the enemy's cavalry, and ridden by one of our hussars, they immediately knew him by his paces, they roused themselves from their stupor, and said to each other, *'Este cavallo es Espanol'*; as if he had been the only cause of our success.

We only passed through Madrid; our regiment being quartered sixteen days at Cevolla, not far from the banks of the Tagus, near Talavera, after which it returned, on the 19th December, to form a part of the garrison of Madrid. The inhabitants of the capital and its neighbourhood had recovered from their great astonishment. By degrees they had become accustomed to the sight of the French. The army observed the strictest discipline; and, at least in appearance, tranquillity was as well established as during a time of peace.

Before entering Madrid by the Toledo gate, the Mançanarés is crossed by a superb stone bridge, sufficiently broad for four carriages to pass abreast with ease. The length of this bridge, and the number and height of its arches, would make one believe at first sight that it was built over a wide river; yet the Mançanarés, exhausted by daily consumption, scarcely flows, and in some places is lost in the sand of its bed. The immense bridges so frequently met with in Spain, and other southern and mountainous countries are necessary because the smallest stream, increased by a sudden influx, is sometimes instantaneously transformed into an impetuous torrent.

There exists in Spain a nobility of cities as well as of men. The Spaniards preserve so much respect for their old institutions, that their capital still bears the name of *villa*, or country town, whereas some poor villages pride themselves on that of *ciudad*, or city, either because they have received this title and the privileges attached to it, as the reward of some great proofs of devotion to their country or sovereign, or inherited it from the ruined towns upon which they themselves are founded. When a Spaniard is asked where he was born, he answers, I am the son of such a town; and this expression, which intimately identifies him with the place of his birth, causes him to attach the more value to the dignity of his native city. Madrid contains no Roman or Moorish monuments; before Charles V it was but a country residence, or *sitio*, where the court passed a few months in the year, as in our days at Aranjuez, the Escurial and St Ildefonso.

One is astonished on entering Madrid by the gate of Toledo and the place of Cevada, where the market is held early in the morning, at the tumultuous concourse of people from the country and the provinces, diversely clothed, going, coming, arriving and departing. Here a Castilian gathers up the ample folds of his cloak with the dignity of a Roman senator wrapped in his toga. There a drover from La Mancha, with a long goad in his hand and clad in a kelt of hide, which also resembles the ancient form of the tunic worn by the Roman and Gothic warriors.

Farther on are seen men whose hair is bound with long silken fillets, and others wearing a sort of short brown vest, chequered with blue and red, which reminds one of the Moresco garb. The men who wear this habit come from Andalusia; they are distinguished by their black lively eyes, their expressive and animated looks, and the rapidity of their utterance. Women sitting in the corners of the streets and in the public places, are occupied preparing food for this passing crowd, whose homes are not in Madrid.

One sees long strings of mules laden with skins of wine or of oil, or droves of asses led by a single man, who talks to them unceasingly. One also meets carriages drawn by eight or ten mules, ornamented with little bells, driven with surprising address by one coachman, either on the trot, or galloping, without reins, and by means of his voice only, using the wildest cries. One long sharp whistle serves to stop all the mules at the same moment. By their slender legs, their tall stature, their proudly raised heads, one would take them for teams of stags or elks. The vociferations of the drivers and the muleteers, the ringing of the church bells, which is unceasing, the various vesture of the men, the superabundance of southern activity, manifested by expressive gesture or shouts in a sonorous language of which we were ignorant, manners so different from our own, all contributed to make the appearance of the capital of Spain strange to men coming from the north, where all goes on so silently. We were so much the more struck with it, as Madrid was the first great town we had found peopled since our entry into Spain.

The inhabitants even of Madrid have all a grave deportment and a measured walk. They wear, as I have already said, large dark-coloured cloaks. The women are in black, and a large black veil covers almost entirely their head and shoulders, which gave rise to the saying among the French soldiers, during the first part of their stay in Madrid, that the city was peopled only by priests and nuns. The women are generally short: they are remarkable rather for the grace and elegance of their figure, than the regularity of their features. Their step is bold and quick, the covering of their feet elegant. A Spanish woman never walks out without her *basquinna* and *mantilla*. The *basquinna* is a black silk or woollen gown made to fit close; the *mantilla* is a large black veil which covers the head and shoulders, and sometimes hides all the face except the eyes and nose. This part of the dress sets off still more the paleness of their complexion and the brilliancy of their eyes. The young women occasionally replace their *mantilla* by an inclination of the head and an easy jerk of the right shoulder and arm. This very graceful motion furnishes them with the opportunity of directing, as if by chance, a look at those who pass or stand by them. The Spanish women keep themselves almost always at home, seated behind their grated balconies. They thence observe all who pass, without being seen, and in the evening listen to guitars, and to tender complaints skilfully expressed in songs. Their rest is sometimes disturbed by the contentions of lovers who walk under their windows in the narrow streets.

At the hour of the siesta, especially in summer, during the heart of the day, all these noises were suspended, the whole city was asleep, and the streets only re-echoed to the trampling of the horses of our corps of calvary going their rounds, or the drum of a solitary detachment mounting guard. This same French drum had beaten the march and the charge in Alexandria, in Cairo, in Rome, and in almost every town in Europe, from Königsberg to Madrid, where we then were.

Before the French began to mix indiscriminately with the population of the city, the inhabitants, male and female, as soon as the evening bell announced the Ave Maria, fell on their knees in the houses, the squares, and even in the middle of the streets; the tumult of life was on a sudden suspended, as if this extensive capital, in which a whole people repeated simultaneously the same prayer, had been for some minutes transformed into one vast temple.

Our regiment remained almost a month in the capital of Spain. I was quartered on an old man of illustrious name, who lived alone with his daughter. He went regularly twice a day to mass, and once to the place Del Sol, to learn the news. He sat down as soon as he came in, in a parlour where he passed his days doing nothing. Sometimes he lighted his segar, and dissipated his cares and his thoughts by smoking: he rarely spoke, and I never saw him laugh. He only exclaimed every half-hour, with a sigh of dejection, '*Ay Jesus!*' his daughter always answered in the same words, and they both again became silent.

A priest, the spiritual director of the house, came every day to see my hosts, with as much assiduity as a physician visits his patients. He wore a fair wig to hide his priest's tonsure, and was habited like an ordinary citizen, always affecting to say that he dared not wear his canonical dress for fear of being murdered by our soldiers. This useless disguise was solely for the purpose of increasing the violent irritation which already existed against the French.

Although, to appearance, the greatest tranquillity prevailed at Madrid, our regiment was always ready to mount at a moment's warning; and our horses, though in the capital, were kept constantly saddled as if it had been an advanced post in presence of the enemy. Eleven hundred determined Spaniards had, according to report, remained concealed in the town when it capitulated, in order to raise the inhabitants and to put an end to every Frenchman at the first favourable opportunity.

The infantry was distributed in the convents of the different quarters of the city: the requisite furniture had not yet been procured, to avoid being troublesome to the inhabitants, and attach them to King Joseph. Our soldiers, subjected in an enemy's country to the strictest discipline, had none of the advantages which compensate the rigour of the military state in regular garrisons. They slept on the cold stone in the long corridors of the monasteries; they were sometimes in want of the necessaries of life, and cursed the poverty of the monks whom they had replaced, gaily complaining, however, of being forced to live like Capuchin friars.

Amidst the strains of victory with which our bulletins resounded, we had a confused feeling of uncertainty concerning the very advantages we had just gained; it might have been said that we had conquered upon volcanos. The Emperor Napoleon made no public entry into Madrid, as he had done into the other capitals of Europe. We were told that he was prevented by the forms imposed by etiquette with regard to his brother Joseph, whom he already considered as a foreign sovereign. Encamped with his guard on the heights of Chamartin, he issued daily decrees to Spain, expecting the immediate submission of that kingdom, from the terror that the rapid success of our arms must have produced.

The thundering proclamations of the Emperor Napoleon announced his triumphs to astonished Europe, and made such parts of the Peninsula as still resisted fear a terrible fate. Nevertheless the provinces of Spain did not seem in any haste to make separate advances towards mollifying the implacable conqueror, and to ward off the fatal blow which they could not but fear. No man presented himself to lay at the feet of Napoleon, along with the required tribute, those obsequious eulogies, to which other countries had accustomed him. The deputations from the city of Madrid, and a few alcades from the places occupied by our troops, came alone to the imperial quarters of Chamartin, to make such submissions as were dictated by fear. Twelve hundred heads of families chosen in Madrid itself were also summoned, and came to take the oath of fidelity to King Joseph. But the priests themselves, had, it is said, absolved them before-hand from all oaths of submission they might make to their conquerors.

The reduction of the religious orders and the abolition of the Inquisition, which had been proclaimed by the French authorities, far from placing them in the light of deliverers, only augmented the violent hatred borne them by the clergy and its numerous followers. The monks of all orders, who had been turned out of the convents, dispersed themselves through the country and preached against us wherever they went. Cloaking their resentment for the recent loss of their revenues under a holy zeal, they sought to excite the people against the French by every possible means. The priests loudly declared that the Inquisition had only been set up against foreigners; and that without the Inquisition, all religious principles would have long been destroyed in Spain, as they had been lost in France, for more than twenty years.

The Inquisition had become much milder during the last century. It no longer inspired the Spaniards with terror, and even enlightened men had come to look upon it as a means necessary to a weak government, in order to curb the people and repress the power of the inferior clergy. The poor began to consider where they should seek, in years of scarcity, that daily food they were accustomed to receive at the convent gates.

This religious people could not conceive how institutions that they regarded as having always existed could ever cease, and in these times of misfortune every change made by an enemy's hand was regarded as impiety.

III

A FEW days after the taking of Madrid, while our regiment was still at Cevolla, on the banks of the Tagus, I received orders to carry an open despatch from General Lassalle, who was in our front at Talavera, to Marshal Lefevre. Marshal Lefevre was to read the despatch and then send it direct to the Prince of Neufchâtel. I met Marshal Lefevre at sunset, just as he arrived from Casa Rubios. In order to spare his own aides-de-camp, the marshal ordered me to go on and to carry the letters I was entrusted with myself to the imperial headquarters. As I was to ride post, I was obliged to leave my horse at Maqueda, and I mounted a *requisition mule*, which the head of the staff forced the alcade of the place to give me.

I was soon on the road, in a dark night, on a vicious mule, whose mane had been cut quite off. A Spanish peasant, who served me as guide, rode before me on a mule the fellow of mine. When we had ridden about a mile my guide fell, and his mule immediately set off on a gallop for his own village. I fancied that the peasant, stunned by his fall, had fainted, and I dismounted to help him, but I sought for him in vain about the place where I heard him fall, he had slipped behind the thick brushwood and disappeared.

I mounted my mule again, not too certain how I was to

57

find my way alone. The restive beast, no longer hearing his companion march before him, would neither go backwards nor forwards. The more I spurred the more he kicked; my blows, my abuse, my threats in French only irritated him the more. I did not know his proper name. I was not even aware that every Spanish mule is provided with one, and that the only way of getting them on, is to say in their own language, 'Go on, mule, get on, Captain, get on, Arragonese,' &c. Having alighted to tighten the girth of my wooden saddle, the provoked mule started to one side and knocked me down with a kick on the breast, then turned into a neighbouring path.

When I recovered from my fall I ran after him with all my strength, guided by the sound of my stirrups, the saddle having turned round and dragging on the stones. When I had run about half a league I found my saddle, which the mule had succeeded in kicking off. I took it on my back, and soon after reached a large village, where the advanced guard of one of Marshal Lefevre's brigades had just arrived. I procured a horse from the alcade and proceeded on my way, taking good care to keep pretty near my guide.

There was no French garrison in the village where I changed horses for the second time. The postmaster opened the door to me himself; he was a spare hale old man. He awoke a postboy, and told him to put my saddle upon an old horse which could hardly stand, his forelegs were so crooked. I began to threaten the postmaster, and, as I raised my voice, pointed at the horse I wanted. The old man was not to be alarmed; he took me by the hand with a tranquillity which instantly disarmed my rage, and, making signs to me to make no noise, he shewed me thirty or forty peasants, asleep upon the cut straw in the barn, at the other end of the stable.

I took his advice, and mounted the bad horse, without saying another word, astonished at the various sentiments indicated by this simple trait, and reflecting on the innumerable difficulties which the hatred of the Spaniards already opposed to us even in the midst of our victories.

At one o'clock in the morning, I arrived at the imperial quarters at Chamartin. The Duke of Neufchâtel was awakened by one of his aides-de-camp. I gave him the letters I had brought, and I was sent back, at eleven o'clock the same night to my own division with fresh despatches for Marshal Victor.

I arrived at Aranjuez in the morning; the commandant of the place advised me to wait, before I went to Toledo, for a detachment which was soon to march. The director of the posts, attached to the first division, had been massacred on the road the evening before, having gone on only a few minutes before his escort. But I had been told, that the orders I was carrying were pressing, and continued my journey, mounted on a small requisition horse. Being alone, I was obliged to perform for myself the offices of rear-guard, advance-guard, and flank, galloping up every eminence, and continually on the watch, for fear of surprise.

The wild horses belonging to the royal stud, mingled with deer and fawns in herds of sixty or seventy head, fled at my approach.

A few miles beyond Aranjuez, I saw, at a distance, two Spanish peasants, who had just fettered a French soldier, and were dragging him into the thicket, to murder him. I rode towards them with all the speed of which my horse was capable, and had the good fortune to arrive time enough to deliver the unhappy prisoner. He was a foot soldier, who had left the hospital at Aranjuez the day before; overcome with fatigue, he had set down while his comrades continued their march. I escorted him to his detachment, which was halting near at hand, and then continued my route.

Nothing can be more horrible than the spectacle which shortly after presented itself before my eyes. At every step I

59

beheld the mutilated bodies of Frenchmen, assassinated during a few previous days, and bloody fragments of clothing strewed up and down. Traces, still recent in the dust, indicated the struggle that some of those wretches had made, and the long tortures they had suffered before they expired. The brazen plates of their military caps were the only marks either of their having once been soldiers, or of the regiments to which they belonged. Those who thus attacked the French on the road to Toledo, were the keepers of the royal stud, and such peasants as had deserted the villages on the arrival of our troops. They had acquired a great ferocity of manners, from the habits of a wandering and solitary life.

I left my dispatches with Marshal Victor, at Toledo, and I returned to my regiment the day before it went to garrison Madrid.

The Spaniards of the plains of Castile already began to recover from the momentary consternation into which our arrival had thrown them. The inhabitants of the places we occupied had retired to the mountains or the woods with their wives and children. From thence they watched all our proceedings, and they lay in ambuscade, near the high roads, to surprise our couriers, and our ordonnance, or to fall suddenly upon such of our detachments as they fancied inferior to them in strength.

Every day we received some disastrous news of the small detachments left in the rear of the army, to maintain the communications. In whatever station we left, as in Germany, posts of correspondence of ten or fifteen men, they were certain of being murdered.

The Spanish Junta had retired to Merida; and thence went to Seville. It had just sent orders to the *alcades* and clergy, even of the places occupied by us, to invite the soldiers belonging to the Spanish militia to rejoin the corps to which they had belonged. These soldiers of their country marched, during the night, through byways to avoid meeting our troops, and thus the dispersed armies of the Spaniards continually recovered from their disasters with inconceivable facility. When the army of Castanos arrived at Cuenca, after the defeat at Tudela, it was reduced to 9,000 foot and 2,000 horse; a month after, at the battle of Ucles, this same army was upwards of 20,000 strong. After the defeat of Blake's army, at Espinosa, the Marquis de la Romana had great difficulty in collecting 5,000 soldiers in Galicia; but, so early as the beginning of December, he had assembled 22,000 men in the neighbourhood of the city of Leon.

Although the Spanish Junta was a weak and ill-settled administration, it possessed, nevertheless, great influence while it seconded the movements originating in the nation itself. These movements were necessarily the more durable as they were entitled voluntary.

The Spanish generals, like their government, had no authority, excepting while they acted in unison with the feelings of those whom they commanded. They could neither restrain their soldiers in success, nor command them when a reverse of fortune occurred, and these undisciplined bands dragged their generals with them in victory or in flight. The pride of the Spaniards was such that they would never attribute their misfortunes to their want of experience or to the military superiority of their enemies: the moment they were beaten, they accused their chiefs of treason. General Saint Juan was hanged by his soldiers at Talavera, General la Penna was superseded by the divisions of Andalusia, and the Duke de l'Infantado forced to take the command of the army at Cuenca.

The Spaniards were a religious and warlike, but not a military people; they even detested and despised everything belonging to regular troops; therefore they were in want of officers, subalterns, and all the means that tend to constitute a well regulated army. They considered the present war as a religious crusade against the French, for their country and their king; and the only military distinction of the greatest part of their citizen soldiers was a red ribbon, with this inscription: *Vincer o morir pro patria et pro Ferdinando septimo*.

At the first call, men from every province presented themselves, almost naked, at the great assemblies which they called their armies. There the ardent desire they had for conquest made them support with admirable patience privations to which all the power of the severest discipline could never have subjected the best regular troops.

Even at the time of our victories, the people of the provinces manifested the greatest incredulity concerning the successes we gained. No Spaniard would believe in the disasters of Spain, or own that she could be conquered. These sentiments, inherent in every mind, rendered the nation invincible, notwithstanding the frequent defeats and individual losses of its armies.

The English had entered Spain towards the end of 1808. Thirteen thousand men, under General Sir David Baird, had landed at Corunna on the 14th of October, and had advanced by Lugo as far as Astorga. Another army of 21,000 men, under General Moore, commander-in-chief of all the British forces, had left Lisbon on the 27th of the same month. It had reached Estremadura and the Castiles, by the roads of Almeida, Ciudad Rodrigo, Alcantara, and Merida. The division which marched by Merida had, on the 22nd of November, advanced as far as the Escurial; all the English corps in the Peninsula were to unite at Salamanca and Valladolid to strengthen the Spanish central army before Burgos. When that army had been dispersed, as well as that of General Blake, in the Asturias, Sir D. Baird retired from

Astorga to Villa Franca; and afterwards, when the French marched upon Madrid, after the affair of Tudela, General Moore recalled the body of English which had reached the Escurial, and concentrated his army in the neigbourhood of Salamanca.

The English armies in Spain remained near a month at Salamanca and Villa Franca, uncertain of what they were to do: they could not advance in the face of the immense forces of the French, nor could they venture to retreat for fear of discouraging the people of Spain, and damping the national spirit which still existed in spite of the greatest misfortunes.

There was a momentary misunderstanding between the Spaniards and English, which occasioned a want of union in their military operations. The Spaniards, forgetting that the English were only auxiliaries in their quarrel, reproached them, first with the slowness of their marches, and soon after with remaining stationary. The English general, in his turn, accused the Spaniards of having constantly concealed from him their situation, and their defeats, and of exaggerating their strength and means of resistance. He was deceived like the leader of the French armies, in the Spanish character, and generally mistook for imbecility the enthusiastic belief and representations of a people without military resources, but strong in patriotism and in their national character, and who are invincible, inasmuch as it is their own determination and spirit which exaggerate their means.

The Spaniards went so far as to persuade themselves that the English meant to leave them to their fate. The French also believed, according to the report generally current, that the English were now only occupied with the means of re-embarking at Corunna and Lisbon. They even sent Marshal Lefevre forward from Talavera to Badajoz, to threaten General Moore's communications, and to force him to return hastily down the Tagus. General Soult, who had remained on the frontiers of Leon, also prepared to enter Galicia; he was to be reinforced by General Junot's corps, which had just arrived from France and was advancing towards Burgos.

Meantime, on the 21st December, it was reported at the imperial headquarters at Chamartin that one of General Franceschi's posts, at Rueda, had been carried during the night, between the 12th and 13th, and that parties of English cavalry were scouring the country, even to the gates of Valladolid.

These advanced parties belonged to General Moore's army, which had quitted Salamanca on the 13th December, and had passed the Douro, to join the 13,000 English whom Sir D. Baird was bringing up from Villa Franca. Their object was to make, in conjunction with Marquis Romana's Spanish troops, an attack upon Marshal Soult, who with 15,000 men occupied the small towns of Guarda, Saldanas and Sahagun, along the little river Cea. On the 21st, a brigade of cavalry belonging to the English advanced guard under General Paget's orders, attacked and defeated a French dragoon regiment which Marshal Soult had left at Sahagun.

On learning this movement of the English, the Emperor Napoleon left Madrid on the 22nd, with his guards and Marshal Ney's corps, to endeavour to cut off their retreat towards Corunna. He reached Villa Castina on the 23rd, Tordesillas on the 25th, Medina de Rio Seco on the 27th, and on the morning of the 29th December his advanced guard, consisting of three squadrons of mounted chasseurs commanded by General Lefevre, presented itself before Benavente, where the English army was.

General Lefevre, finding the bridge over the Esla broken down, forded that river, and drove in the English advanced posts to the gates of the city. The General, hurried on by the eagerness of pursuit, forgot to form his chasseurs, and to send on scouts; he was soon engaged with the cavalry of the enemy's rearguard. The French chasseurs were forced to repass the Esla; sixty men, wounded or dismounted, among whom was the General, remained in the hands of the English.

The French chasseurs rallied and formed on the opposite bank of the river, and were preparing to make a desperate charge to recover their chief, when the English brought two pieces of light artillery to bear near the broken bridge, and with grape-shot, forced the French squadrons to retire.

The Anglo-Spanish armies learnt of the march of the Emperor Napoleon at the moment they were preparing to attack Marshal Soult at the village of Carion: they began to retire rapidly, on the 24th, upon Astorga and Benavente, by the roads of Mayorga, Valencia, and Mancilla. They would probably have been cut off from the passes of Galicia, if the French army had not been considerably impeded in its march by the snow recently fallen in the sierra of Guadarama, and by the torrents which had overflowed.

On the 30th December, the Emperor Napoleon arrived at Benavente; he went no farther than Astorga, but returned on the 7th January with his guards; and a few days afterwards he was in France, making preparations for marching against Austria.

Marshal Ney remained at Astorga, to guard the passes of Galicia and to organize the country: Marshal Soult continued to pursue General Moore's army towards Corunna. The country the English left behind them in their retreat was totally wasted, and every night Marshal Soult's troops had to seek provisions at very great distances from the beaten road, which considerably retarded their march and augmented their fatigues. Nevertheless the advanced guards of Marshal Soult's army, first at Villa Franca and afterwards at Lugo, reached the enemy's reserve, but were not strong enough to attack it. It was in an engagement which took place before the first of these towns, that the French lost General Colbert, of the cavalry.

On the 16th, the English were forced to give battle at Corunna, before they embarked; the business was bloody and well contested. The French at first gained ground, but, towards the end of the day, the English recovered the strong position in which they had placed themselves, to cover the anchorage of their fleet, and they embarked during the night, between the 16th and 17th. General Moore was struck by a cannon ball at the moment when he was leading a corps, which had been broken, back to the charge.

The army of the Marquis de la Romana had dispersed itself among the mountains, to the westward of Astorga. The town of Corunna, surrounded by fortifications, was defended by its inhabitants, and only capitulated on the 20th. The English troops had suffered, in their retreat, all the evils to which armies hotly pursued are exposed, when the soldiers are exasperated beyond endurance by fatigue; and, without having ever fought a pitched battle, they had lost more than 10,000 men, their treasure, a great deal of baggage, and almost all their horses.

It is not easy to imagine the causes which induced General Moore to risk his whole army, by an expedition against Marshal Soult,* the result of which could only be extremely

---

*These causes are sufficiently known to the English reader; yet it is impossible for the translator, who has the honour to call Sir John Moore a countryman, to pass over this passage without a protest against any censure, or implied censure, conveyed in Mr Rocca's pages; and without entreating the reader to turn to the narrative of Sir John Moore's campaign, where the griefs and vexations of that noble heart are recorded, and the bright page of his military career laid open for the admiration and example of his countrymen. – (*Translator's note.*)

doubtful, as the Marshal might have retired upon Burgos, and have been reinforced by General Junot's corps. By going towards Saldanas, General Moore gave the Emperor Napoleon, who was preparing to return to France, an opportunity of attacking him with the whole of his united forces.

From Salamanca, General Moore might have thrown himself behind the bridge of Almarez, over the Tagus, into an almost impregnable situation, where he could have reorganized the Spanish armies. It was there that he was most dreaded by the French. At all events, on leaving Salamanca, General Moore should have retired rather upon Lisbon than on Corunna, to shorten his own road, while he increased the difficulties of Marshals Lefevre and Soult, by widening the communications they had to maintain, and thus forcing them to weaken themselves, by leaving behind them a greater number of detachments. The English general would thus have furnished the troops of General Romana and the peasants of Galicia and Portugal with numerous opportunities of carrying on a petty war against the French detachments. This last operation has been performed since with the greatest success by General Sir Arthur Wellesley.

It is asserted, that General Moore was deceived by false reports, and that it was against his own judgment and wishes that he was induced on this occasion to overstep the rules of military science. For the rest, it is always easy to judge of things when the event is known; the difficulty in all enterprises is to foresee this probable result.

While Marshal Soult was driving the English from Galicia, the Spanish army of Andalusia was making divers movements in advance from Cuenca, apparently threatening Madrid; and Marshal Victor set out on the 10th January from Toledo with the first corps to oppose that army, commanded by the Duke de l'Infantado.

The first division was several days in the neighbourhood of Ocana, advancing slowly, without receiving any news of the enemy. Either by chance or from ignorance of the ground, the French found themselves, on the morning of the 13th, so completely engaged in the very midst of the Spaniards that, without having the smallest intention of attempting to turn them, they imagined themselves to be surrounded.

Villate's division was the first to engage with a part of the enemy's army, drawn up in battle array on the summit of a high and steep hill. The Spaniards confided more in the strength of their position than in the experience of their troops, which were chiefly new recruits. When they saw the vigour and coolness with which the French, under arms, climbed the rocks, they dispersed as soon as they had fired their first volley, and in retreating, at a short distance from Alcazar, they met Ruffin's division, which, in pursuit of the enemy, had turned them without being aware of it.

Several thousand Spaniards were obliged to throw down their arms. Terror seized their whole army, and the various corps which composed it precipitately fled on all sides. Several of the enemy's columns, in attempting to escape, came upon General Cenarmont's park of artillery, and were received by a discharge of grapeshot, which forced them to change their direction. A French piece of artillery, the horses of which were much fatigued, was met on the road by the enemy's cavalry, who opened and filed off in silence on each side of the road. The French made more than 2,000 prisoners, and took forty pieces of cannon, which the Spaniards left behind in their flight. If General Latour Maubourg's division of dragoons had not been too much fatigued to follow the enemy, the whole Spanish army must have fallen into the hands of the French.

The 13th January, the day on which the affair of Ucles took place, our regiment left Madrid, to join the first division of the army. On the 14th, we lay at Ocana; and, at three leagues distance from that city, on the morning of the 15th, we met the Spanish prisoners coming from Ucles, on their way to Madrid; many of these wretches sunk under their fatigue, others died of inanition; when they could march no farther, they were shot without mercy.

This sanguinary order was given by way of reprisal against the Spaniards, who hanged such Frenchmen as they took prisoners. Such violent measures, taken at an unfavourable moment against disarmed enemies whose very weakness should have protected them, could not in any case be justified by the necessity of reprisal. Besides, these measures, as impolitic as they were cruel, retarded the real end of the proposed conquest, which was the lasting subjection of the vanquished nation. It is true, that the Spanish peasants were thus prevented from joining the armies, but the result was that a war of ambuscades took place of open battles, in which our eminent superiority in tactics would probably always have given us means of conquering our enemies, and we might afterwards have subjected by gentle means men already half-reclaimed by military discipline. The French were destined, with only 400,000 men, to struggle against twelve millions of beings, animated by hatred, despair, and revenge.

One of the unfortunate Spanish prisoners particularly attracted our attention; he was stretched on his back, mortally wounded; his long black mustachios, sprinkled with a few grey hairs, and his uniform, marked him for an old soldier. His nearly inarticulate words seemed to invoke the Virgin and the Saints; we endeavoured to revive him with a little brandy, but he died in a few moments.

Nothing is more dreadful than to follow a few marches behind a victorious army. As we had had no share in the success of our comrades, who had just beaten the enemy in our front, we had no remembrance of our own dangers,

69

fatigues, or anxieties, to weaken the horrible effect of the scene which presented itself at every step. We traversed a wasted and deserted country; we lodged indiscriminately among the dead and the dying, who had dragged their wounded limbs through the mud of the field of battle, to die, without help, in the nearest hovels.

At Cuenca we joined our division, and for some days we occupied cantonments at Belmonte and the neighbourhood of San Clemente. We waited for our artillery, which had great difficulty in advancing even one league, or at most two, in a day: the winter rains had so destroyed the roads that it was frequently necessary to use the horses belonging to several pieces of cannon to drag a single gun.

We afterwards crossed the country of Don Quixote, on our way to Consuegra and Madrilejos. Toboso perfectly answers the description of Cervantes, in his immortal poem of *Don Quixote de la Mancha*. If that imaginary hero was not of any great service to widows and orphans during his lifetime, his memory at least protected the supposed country of his Dulcinea from some of the horrors of war. As soon as the French soldiers saw a woman at a window, they cried out, laughingly, 'There's Dulcinea!'

Their gaiety tranquillised the inhabitants; far from flying, as usual, at the first sight of our advanced posts, they crowded to see us pass; witticisms upon Dulcinea and Don Quixote became a bond of union between our soldiers and the inhabitants of Toboso, and the French, being well received, treated their hosts in return with civility.

We remained near a month quartered in La Mancha. Whether in houses, or bivouacked in the fields, we led the same sort of life, either going from house to house, or from our own fire in the open air to that of a comrade. In either situation, we passed the long nights in drinking and talking over the present events of the war, or our past campaigns. Sometimes, a horse, tormented by the chilliness of the dews just before daybreak, would tear up the picket to which he was fastened, and come gently and put his head close to the fire to warm himself, as if he was conscious of being an old servant, and wished to remind us that he also been present in the battle.

The simple, yet agitated, life we led had its evils and its charms. When in presence of the enemy, at every hour of the day detachments were seen departing or returning after a long absence, and bringing news of other parties in the most distant and various parts of Spain. When we received orders to be ready to mount, we were equally ignorant of our destination; it might have been France, Germany, the farthest extremity of Europe, or only a short ride. When we took leave of each other, we knew not if we should ever meet again. When we halted, we could not tell whether it was only for a few hours, or for whole months.

Even the longest and most monotonous residence in one place passed without ennui, because we had always the chance of an unforeseen occurrence. We were often in absolute want of the necessaries of life, but we consoled ourselves in our distress by hopes of a speedy change. When we came to plenty, we made haste to enjoy it; we lived as fast as we could, because we knew that nothing could last long. When the cannon roared at a distance, announcing an approaching attack, on any point of the enemy's line; when the different corps were hurrying into action, brothers and friends serving in several divisions recognized each other and stopped to embrace, and had a hasty farewell; their arms clashed, their plumes crossed each other, and they returned instantly to their ranks.

The habit of danger made us look upon death as one of the most ordinary circumstances of life; we pitied our comrades when wounded, but when once they had ceased to live, the indifference which was shewn them amounted almost to irony.

71

When, as the soldiers passed by, they recognized one of their companions stretched among the dead, they just said, 'He is in want of nothing, he will not have his horse to abuse again, he has got drunk for the last time,' or something similar, which only marked in the speaker a stoical contempt of existence. Such were the only funeral orations pronounced in honour of those who fell in our battles.

The various troops that composed our army, especially the cavalry and infantry, differed extremely in manners and habits. The foot soldiers, having only to think of themselves and their guns, were selfish, great talkers, and great sleepers. Condemned during a campaign by the fear of dishonour, to march boldly up to death, they shewed themselves merciless in battle, and whenever they could inflicted on others the sufferings which themselves had borne. They were apt to dispute with their officers, and sometimes they were even insolent to them; but in the midst of the dreadful fatigues they had to support, a *bon mot* put them in good humour, and brought them over to the laugher's side. They forgot all their hardships the moment they heard the sound of the enemy's first gun.

The hussars and chasseurs were generally accused of being plunderers and prodigal, loving drink and fancying every thing fair while in presence of the enemy. Accustomed, one may almost say, to sleep with an open eye, to have an ear always awake to the sound of the trumpet, to reconnoitre far in advance during a march, to trace the ambuscades of the enemy, to observe the slightest traces of their marches, to examine defiles, and to scan the plains with eagle sight, they could not fail to have acquired superior intelligence and habits of independence. Nevertheless, they were always silent and submissive in presence of their officers, for fear of being dismounted.

Forever smoking, to pass away his life, the light horseman, under his large cloak, braved in every country the rigour of the seasons. The rider and his horse, accustomed to live together, contracted a character of resemblance. The rider derived animation from his horse, and the horse from his rider. When a hussar, not quite sober, pressed his horse to speed, in ravines or among precipices, the horse assumed the empire which reason might before have given to the man; he restrained his spirit, redoubled his caution, avoided danger, and always returned, after a few turnings, to take his own and his master's place in the ranks. Sometimes also, during a march, the horse would gently slacken his pace, or lean on one side or the other, to keep his intoxicated and sleeping master in the saddle; and when the involuntary sleep was over, and the hussar saw his horse panting his fatigue, he would weep, and swear never to drink more. For several days he would march on foot, and would go without his own bread to feed his companion.

When a carabine shot from the videttes gave the alarm in a camp of light cavalry, every horse was saddled in an instant, and the French horsemen were seen on every side leaping over the fires of the bivouac, the hedges, the ditches, and with the rapidity of lightning flying to the place of rendezvous to repel the first attack of the enemy. The trumpeter's horse alone remained impassive in the midst of the tumult, but the moment his master had ceased to blow, he pawed the ground with impatience and hastened to join his comrades.

Our division quitted La Mancha towards the middle of February, and the troops under the command of General Sebastiani, who had succeeded Marshal Lefevre, came to the environs of Toledo, in order to observe the remains of the Duke de l'Infantado's army. We proceeded to occupy Talavera, Arzobispo, and Almarez, on the right bank of the Tagus, in face of the Spanish army of Estremadura. That army had been dispersed on the 24th of December, by

73

Marshal Lefevre, at Arzobispo, and opposite Almarez; it had since recovered itself, and been reinforced under the command of General Cuesta; it had retaken the bridge of Almarez from the French, and had blown up the principal arches, which completely arrested the march of our troops and put us under the absolute necessity of constructing a new bridge over the Tagus, under the enemy's fire. It is true, we had two other bridges at Arzobispo and at Talavera, but the roads by them were at that time impassable for cannon.

Marshal Victor fixed his headquarters at the village of Almarez, that he might be in a situation to defend the works, and to superintend the construction of rafts. A part of our division of light horse went over to the left bank over the river to observe the enemy and to reconnoitre their right flank, which was stationed on the Ibor.

We often changed our quarters, on account of the difficulty of procuring forage and provisions. The inhabitants had abandoned almost the whole country occupied by the army. Before their departure, they frequently walled up all that they could not carry with them. Our soldiers, having discovered this, were in the habit of measuring like architects the outer dimensions of the empty houses, and then the inner apartments, to discover if any space had been thus taken from them. They also frequently found jars of wine buried in the earth. We were thus accustomed to live by chance, as it were, passing whole weeks without bread, and even without being able to procure barley for our horses.

At length, on the 14th March, our rafts were finished, but we could neither launch them, nor construct a bridge under the enemy's fire, and it was found necessary to drive them from their strong position opposite to Almarez, at the confluence of the Tagus and Ibor.

On the 15th March, a party from the first division crossed the Tagus, at Talavera and at Arzobispo, to fall upon the flank and rear of the Spanish posts. The German division, under General Leval, attacked the enemy, on the morning of the 17th, at Messa de Ibor; 3,000 of that division, without its artillery, overthrew with the bayonet 8,000 Spaniards, entrenched on a high hill, and defended by six pieces of cannon. The whole of the 18th was employed in driving the enemy from Valdecannar, and in pursuing him from post to post, and from rock to rock, as far as the gulley of Miravette. Our regiment was with Villate's division, on the left wing of the army. We went up the banks of the Ibor, having no difficulty in driving the Spaniards from every point, as they never stood when they found their positions turned.

On the 19th March, the whole army remained stationary, while the rafts were launched. The flying bridge being finished before night, the artillery, and the troops which had remained on the right bank of the Tagus, began to pass on the same day. On the 20th, the whole army assembled at Truxillo. A little before our arrival, there had been an engagement between the mounted chasseurs of the 5th Regiment, who composed our advanced guard, and the royal carabineers of the enemy's rearguard, before that city. The number of killed on both sides was nearly equal. The Spaniards lost a field officer.

The two armies passed the night in sight of each other: an hour before sunrise next day, the enemy marched, and we followed soon after. The 10th Chasseurs formed the advanced guard of our division of light horse, which itself cleared the way for the whole of the army. Four companies of light infantry passed on before us, whenever we came to a mountainous or woody country.

Two hours before sunset, the advanced corps of the 10th Chasseurs reached the enemy's rearguard, which, finding itself close pressed, immediately retired upon the main body of the Spanish army. The colonel of the 10th allowed himself to be carried away by too much ardour, and imprudently permitted his whole regiment to charge; it became animated, and pursued the Spanish cavalry for more than a league, along a causeway between rocky hills, planted with ilex.

When a regiment or a squadron of cavalry charges in line or in column, it cannot long maintain the order in which it sets out; the horses animate one another, their eagerness progressively increases, and the best mounted horsemen generally find themselves far before the others, which breaks the order of battle. The commander of an advanced corps should be careful not to make long charges, and should frequently form his lines, in order to let the horses take breath and to have time to reconnoitre for fear of ambuscades. Besides, at all events, when one is too far advanced to receive timely help from another body, it is right to keep at least half the corps in reserve, to sustain the other, and to form for the attacking party a sort of rampart behind which they may rally, if they should be repulsed and followed by a superior force.

Not far from the village of Mia Casas, the Spaniards had placed several squadrons of their best cavalry in ambush; this chosen cavalry fell unawares upon the chasseurs of our advanced guard, who were marching without order and separate, at considerable intervals behind each other. Our horsemen were overpowered by numbers: their horses, fatigued by an excessive long charge, could not form to resist, and, in less than ten minutes, our enemies completely destroyed upwards of 150 of the bravest of our 10th Regiment.

General Lasalle, as soon as he learnt what had happened, sent us on hastily to assist them. We arrived too late; we saw nothing but the cloud of dust at a distance, which the retiring Spaniards left behind them.

The colonel of the 10th was endeavouring to rally his

chasseurs, and tearing his hair at the sight of the wounded strewed here and there over a pretty considerable space of ground. Night coming on, we returned to bivouac, a little in the rear of the spot where the action had taken place.

On the 22nd March, the enemy crossed the Guadiana. We took up various quarters in the neighbourhood of San Pedro and Mia Casas, and our artillery at length coming up, on the 23rd the greater part of the army concentrated itself in the town of Merida, and its neighbourhood.

During the night, between the 27th and 28th, the whole army was in motion, to march towards the enemy. General Cuesta had been several days in the plains before Medellin, awaiting us; his engineers had reconnoitred, beforehand, the advantageous position in which he placed his army.

The Spaniards, to whom pitched battles had been so often fatal, sought, by every means, to procure that confidence of which they were in want. They looked upon the skirmish of Mia Casas as a lucky omen. They also dwelt on an ancient superstition, attached to the memory of the victories gained by their ancestors over the Moors, in these very plains, on the banks of the Guadiana. The French required no ground for their hopes, they trusted from habit to victory.

On crossing the Guadiana, over a very long and narrow bridge, one enters Medellin; on the other side of which is an immense plain, without trees, which extends along the Guadiana upwards, between the river, the town of Don Benito, and the village of Mingabril. At first, the Spaniards had occupied the heights which separate these two places; afterwards they spread their line, and formed a kind of crescent, their left at Mingabril, their centre in front opposite to Don Benito, and their right wing near the Guadiana.

At eleven o'clock in the morning we left Medellin, to place ourselves in order of battle; at a little distance from the town we formed an arc of a very narrow circle, between

the Guadiana and a ravine planted with trees and vine-
yards, extending from Medellin to Mingabril. General
Lasalle's division of light cavalry was placed on the left, in
the centre the division of German infantry, and on the right
General Latour Maubourg's dragoons: Villate and Ruffin's
divisions were in reserve. The three divisions which formed
our first line of battle had left numerous detachments in the
rear to keep up our communications, so that we had scarcely
7,000 soldiers. The enemy before us presented an immense
front, more than 34,000 strong.

The body of Germans began the attack; the 2nd and 4th
Regiments of Dragoons having next charged the Spanish
infantry, they were repulsed with loss, and the Germans
remained alone in the midst of the battle; they formed a
square, and, during the rest of the action, vigorously
resisted every effort of the enemy. With much difficulty
Marshal Victor renewed the fight, by bringing up two regiments of Villate's division. The enemy's horse first tried in
vain to break our right wing; a large body of it then fell at
once upon our left, which, for fear of being surrounded,
was forced to make a retrograde movement upon the
Guadiana, where it forms an elbow and straightens the
plain towards Medellin. We retired for two hours slowly and
silently, stopping every fifty paces to face about and present
our front to the enemy, in order to dispute our ground with
him before we abandoned it, whenever he attempted to
drive us from it.

In the midst of the whizzing of the bullets, and the
deeper sound of the bombs, which, after cutting through
the air, ploughed up the earth around us, the voices of the
officers alone were heard; the closer the enemy pressed, the
more coolly and collectedly did they give their orders.

As we retired, the cries of the Spaniards redoubled; their
skirmishers were so numerous and so bold, that they frequently forced ours back to their ranks. They shouted to us

from afar, in their own tongue, that they would give no quarter, and that the plains of Medellin should be the grave of the French. Had our squadron been broken and dispersed, the Spanish horse of the right would have burst through the opening, on the rear of our army, and surrounded it; the plains of Medellin would then, indeed, have become, as our enemies hoped, the grave of the French.

General Lasalle rode proudly and calmly backwards and forwards in front of his division. When the enemy's cavalry came within gunshot, the skirmishers on each side retired, and in the space which separated us from the Spaniards, nothing was seen but the horses of the dead, both friends and enemies, running wounded about the plain, some of them struggling to get rid of the cumbersome burden of their masters, whom they were dragging with them.

The Spaniards had sent six chosen squadrons against our single one; they marched in close column; at their head were the lancers of Xeres. This whole body began at once to quicken their pace, in order to charge us while we were retiring. The captain commanding our squadron made his four platoons, who together were only 120 strong, wheel half round to the right. This movement being made, he adjusted the front line of his troop as quietly as if we had not been in presence of the enemy. The Spanish horse, seized with astonishment at his coolness, involuntarily slackened their pace. Our commandant profited by their momentary hesitation, and ordered the charge to be sounded.

Our hussars, who in the midst of the threats and abuse of the enemy had preserved the strictest silence, then drowned the sound of the trumpet as they moved onwards, by a single and terrible shout of joy and fury. The Spanish lancers stopped; seized with terror, they turned their horses at the distance of half pistol-shot, and overthrew their own cavalry, which was behind them. Terror had taken such hold of them that they dared not look on each other for fear of seeing an enemy. Our hussars mingled with them indiscriminately, cut them down without resistance, and we followed them to the rear of their own army. Our trumpets now sounding the recall, we abandoned the enemy to return and form our line again. A little after our charge, the whole of the Spanish cavalry, both right and left, entirely disappeared.

Our dragoons had rallied round their picked companies; they took advantage of the uncertainty of the Spanish infantry, which seemed shaken by the flight of the cavalry, and made against the Spanish centre a brilliant and fortunate charge. Two regiments of Villate's division attacked the enemy's infantry on the right with success, at the same moment, near the heights of Mingabril.

In an instant the army that was before us disappeared, like clouds driven by the wind. The Spaniards threw down their arms and fled; the cannonade ceased, and the whole of our cavalry went off in pursuit of the enemy.

Our soldiers, who had seen themselves threatened with certain death, had they sunk under the number of their foes, and irritated by five hours' resistance, gave no quarter at first. The infantry followed the cavalry at a distance, and dispatched the wounded with the bayonet. The fury of our soldiers was particularly directed against such Spaniards as were without military dresses.

The hussars and dragoons, who had dispersed themselves as foraging parties, soon came back, driving in immense bodies of Spaniards, whom they delivered up to the infantry to conduct to Medellin. The same men who had confidently promised us death before the battle now marched with downcast looks, and with the precipitation of fear. At the first sign or menace of our people, they crowded together towards the middle of their columns, like sheep when they hear the voice of pursuing dogs. Every time they met any French troops they cried aloud, 'Long live Napoleon and his invincible troops!' Sometimes, too, one or two horsemen passing by amused themselves with extorting the acclamations which were only due to the whole body of the conquerors.

A certain colonel, who was a courtier and an aide-de-camp, and who was looking on as the prisoners passed in files before our regiments, ordered them to to shout, in Spanish '*Viva il Re Joseph!*' The prisoners at first appeared not to understand, then, after a moment's silence, they all together repeated the cry of 'Long live Napoleon and his invincible troops!'

The colonel then seized on an individual prisoner, and repeated the order with threats. The prisoner having then shouted, '*Viva Joseph!*' a Spanish officer, who, according to custom, had not been disarmed, came up to his country-man and ran his sword through his body. Our enemies had no objection to pay homage to our victorious arms, but they could never be brought to acknowledge the authority of a master not of their own choice, even in their lowest fortune.

I returned to the town of Medellin a little before night. Silence and quiet had succeeded to the activity of battle, and the shouts of victory. In the plain, the only audible sounds were the groans of the wounded, and the confused murmurs of the dying, as they raised their heads in prayer to God and the blessed Virgin. On every individual with whom the ground was strewed, death had stamped the expression of the passion which had animated him at the moment of his fall. Those who had been struck in their flight, were lying on their faces or their sides, their heads sunk upon their breasts, and terror seemed to have con-tracted every muscle. Those on the contrary, who had met death bravely fighting, had preserved, even in their death, an air of pride.

Two regiments of Swiss and Walloon guards were stretched on the field in the very line they had occupied in battle. Some broken ammunition waggons, cannon, with their teams of mules, left to themselves, still marked the position which the Spanish army had occupied. Here and there lay wounded horses, whose legs being broken by the shot, could not stir from the spot on which they were soon to perish. Ignorant of death, and equally so of futurity, they lay grazing on the field as far as their necks could reach.

The French did not lose 4,000 men. The Spaniards left on the field 12,000 dead, and nineteen pieces of artillery; we made seven or 8,000 prisoners, but of these scarcely 2,000 reached Madrid. In their own country, the Spanish prisoners found it very easy to escape.

The inhabitants of the towns and villages assembled in great numbers on their road, to distract the attention of the French escorts; they took care to leave their doors open, and the prisoners mingled in the crowd as they passed, and ran into the houses, whose doors readily shut to save them. Our French soldiers, who recovered their humanity after the battle was over, lent themselves to these practices, notwithstanding the severity of their orders on the subject.

The Spanish prisoners would say with a sigh, as they pointed out a distant village, to a grenadier who had to guard and lead them, 'Senor Soldado – Mr Soldier – there is our native village; there are our wives and children. Must we pass so near them without ever seeing them again? Must we go so far off as France?'

The grenadier would answer, affecting a rough manner, 'If you attempt to escape I shoot you, such are my orders, but I never see behind me.'

He would then march forward, the prisoners would take to the fields, and soon rejoin their armies. Latterly, we were obliged to send German escorts with our prisoners; their national character and strict discipline rendered them vigilant and inflexible.

A part of our regiment was left at Mingabril, on the field of the battle of Medellin, near the place where the engagement had been hottest. We lived in the midst of the dead, and we hourly saw the dark thick vapours rise, which, impelled forwards by the winds, spread pestilence and infection in the surrounding country. The oxen of La Mesta, who had come as usual to winter on the banks of the Guadiana, fled with horror from their accustomed pastures. Their melancholy lowings, and the long howls of the dogs who kept them, indicated the vague instinct of terror which agitated them.

Thousands of enormous vultures had assembled from every part of Spain over the vast and silent field of death; placed on heights, and seen from a distance against the horizon, they appeared as large as men. Our videts often marched towards them to reconnoitre, mistaking them for enemies. They never left their human prey on our approach, till we were within a few paces of them, and then the flapping of their enormous wings echoed far and wide over our heads, like a funeral knell.

IV

ON THE 27th March, two days before the battle of Medellin or Merida, General Sebastiani had completely defeated the Spanish army destined to guard the passes of the Sierra Morena, near Ciudad Real, in La Mancha. This victory, together with that we had just gained at Medellin, spread consternation over all Andalusia, every road through which remained for the moment open to the French.

The Spanish government, however, did not allow itself to be depressed by these two great misfortunes; like the Roman senate, which, after the defeat at Cannæ, thanked Varus because he had not despaired of the salvation of Rome, the supreme junta of Seville declared by a public ordonnance that Cuesta and his army had deserved well of their country, and awarded to them the same recompense as if they had been victorious. In such desperate circumstances, to blame Cuesta and his army would have been to have owned themselves conquered.

A fortnight after the battle of Medellin, the Spanish army recovered from its losses, and with a force of 30,000 men had occupied the passes of the mountains in our front. General Sebastiani did not advance farther into La Mancha than Santa Cruz de la Mudella, and our corps remained quartered between the Tagus and Guadiana. We dared not advance very far from the latter river, lest we should expose ourselves to having our only communication with Madrid, by the bridge of Almarez, cut off by new bodies of Spaniards, which were ready to form in our rear. Besides, it was a long time since we had heard of Marshal Soult's army, which was to have entered Portugal, and with which we were to co-operate and to unite our right wing.

The French army in the north of the Peninsula had not met with success equal to that which we had gained, by the superiority of our discipline, in the plains of Estremadura and La Mancha. The troops under the orders of Marshals Soult and Ney had had to fight in a mountainous country, where the inhabitants had it constantly in their power by their local knowledge, their activity and their numbers to baffle the calculations of military science and the consummate experience of two of the most renowned of our chiefs.

After the retreat of General Moore and the capitulation of Corunna and Ferrol in the month of January, Marshal Soult marched towards Portugal by San Jago, Vigo and Tuy; but his army not being able to cross the Minho near its mouth, exposed to the fire of the fortresses on the opposite bank which belonged to the Portuguese, he reascended the river to Orense, where he crossed the Minho on the 6th March; on the 7th, on the heights of Orsuma near Monte Rey he completely defeated the army of the Marquis of Romana, and drove its remains into the high mountains near Pinbla de Senabria.

On the 13th, Marshal Soult invested Chaves, a frontier town of Portugal, and took it by capitulation; on the 19th he entered Braga, after having forced the defile of Carvalho d'Este, one of the most formidable positions of Portugal. At length, on the 29th March Oporto, defended by an entrenched camp and by 270 pieces of cannon, was carried by assault by the body of Marshal Soult's army, and the vanguard of this body passed the Douro and proceeded to the Vouga, forty-five leagues from Lisbon.

Scarcely had the French made their victorious entrance into Oporto than the garrisons which they had left behind them to keep possession of the country and their communication open were taken on all parts.

The Portuguese troops in the fortress of Caminha, placed at the mouth of the Minho, had crossed the river since the 10th March, and had now joined a considerable number of Spanish marines and of inhabitants from the coast of Galicia, who had taken arms under the orders of their priests. They had fortified the bridge of San Payo against the French, who could have come by San Jago, and had also made themselves masters, by capitulation, of the town of Vigo. Chaves was also retaken on the 21st March by the Portuguese general Francisco Silveira, who had first retreated to Villa-Pouca on the approach of the French; this general, after the taking of Chaves, advanced to Amarante on the Tamega to hold this strong position, from whence he might harass the rearguard and the French detachments in the environs of Oporto.

On the 30th March, Romana descended from the mountains of Puebla de Sanabria, with some thousands of his men, the wreck of his beaten army, and proceeding to Ponteferrada took a small number of French prisoners. He found there some ammunition and provisions, and retook a single damaged 12-pounder; repaired it, crossed the route of Castile; possessed himself, by the aid of his single cannon, of Villa Franca, and made the garrison prisoners; it held 800 men. On the news of this slight success, his army soon swelled, as the ball of snow enlarges itself in descending the mountains and at length becomes an avalanche. Romana forced Marshal Ney to abandon Brezzo, to concentrate himself on Lugo; Romana then threw himself in the Asturias, which he stirred up to arms as he had done Galicia.

The two French bodies of Galicia and Portugal, cut off

from all means of communication, were then entirely insulated; and, separated from the other armies, they could no
longer assist each other, nor cooperate for the common
end of the general operations of the war, and thus they
exhausted themselves from that moment, in a series of partial actions without any result.

Marshal Ney in vain tried to force Galicia to submission
by the terror of his arms. Violent measures, far from keeping down the inhabitants, only sharpened their hatred of
the French, and, what always happens in a country where
there is patriotism, violent measures led to reprisals still
more violent. Squadrons, entire battalions, were annihilated by the peasants in the course of a night. Seven hundred French prisoners were drowned at once in the Minho
by order of Don Pedro de Barrios, Governor of Galicia for
the Junta; and the fury of the inhabitants, far from dimin-
ishing, was every day increased by the growing weakness of
the French army.

The inhabitants of Portugal had risen in mass like those
of Galicia, and the Portuguese opposed the French with
12,000 soldiers of the line, and 70,000 of their militia.
Marshal Soult could not with only 22,000 men keep the
country in his rear and advance to Lisbon. He remained,
however, more than forty days in Oporto, trying in vain to
make the inhabitants submit, and to re-establish his intercepted communications; he had not received for several
months either orders or reinforcements.

Notwithstanding the danger of his situation, he did not
make a retrograde movement, fearful that by this he might
injure the operations of the other bodies of our armies,
of whose positions he remained completely ignorant. At
length, he resolved on the 2nd May that the division of
General Loison should take the bridge of Amaranta on the
Tamega, preparing to retire from Portugal on the route of
Braganza.

During these transactions, the outposts of the French on the Vouga were attacked by the English, and they recrossed the Douro on the following day. The English army, which had returned to Portugal after the retreat of General Moore, was reduced to 15,000 men; it had not at first ventured to disembark its heavy baggage, holding itself ready to re-embark on the first approach of the French. The 4th and the 22nd April it had received considerable reinforcements, and, more than 23,000 strong, it approached Oporto.

The French quitted this city the 12th May, and their rear had an affair with the advance guard of the English. The army of Marshal Soult was pursued and encircled by three hostile armies; that of General Sir A. Wellesley, who never lost sight of the French rearguard; the Anglo-Portuguese army of General Beresford, who marched by Lamego and Amaranta, on Chaves, advancing by several marches on the right of Marshal Soult; and the Portuguese of General Francisco Silveira, in advance of the two first, that he might cut the French off from the passes of Ruivaes between Salamonde and Montalegre.

Marshal Soult, finding the route of Chaves occupied by Marshal Beresford, rapidly concentrated his army on Braga, and directed his march to Orense by the difficult roads of the mountains: he lost, in traversing these insurgent tracts, a third of his *corps d'armée*, and was obliged to abandon all his heavy baggage and artillery.

The English did not advance beyond Montalegre and Chaves; they returned quickly on the Tagus, towards the environs of Lisbon. Marshal Soult arrived on the 22nd May at Lugo in Galicia, relieved the garrison of this town, who were besieged by the Spaniards, and opened a communication with Marshal Ney, who had returned from an expedition against Oviedo in the Asturias. A few days after he recommenced hostilities with the army of the Marquis of Romana, whom he pursued without effect, by Monforte,

Ponteferrada, Bollo, and Viana. He then proceeded, by Puebla de Sanabria, to Zamora, leaving Galicia, with a design to follow the movement which the English, it seemed to him, were making towards the Tagus in Estremadura, against the army of Marshal Victor.

After the departure of Marshal Soult, Marshal Ney was soon forced to retire into the kingdom of Leon. His army had made no durable establishment in Galicia and in the Asturias, having been constantly hindered by the inhabitants of villages, and by numerous troops of armed peasants, which it was impossible to reduce, for the number was every day increasing.

In these mountainous provinces of the north of the Peninsula, the French, although always conquerors where the Spaniards and Portuguese showed themselves in battle, were not however the less assailed by clouds of armed mountaineers, who, never coming near to fight in close ranks, or body to body, retreated from position to position, from rock to rock, on heights, without ceasing to fire, even in flying.

It sometimes required entire battalions to carry an order of a battalion to another distant one. The soldiers wounded, sick, or fatigued, who remained behind the French columns, were immediately murdered. Every victory produced only a new conflict. Victories had become useless, by the persevering and invincible character of the Spaniards; and the French armies were consuming themselves, for want of repose, in continual fatigues, nightly watchings, and anxieties.

Such were the events which had passed in the north of Spain, and which had hindered our armies of Estremadura and La Mancha from profiting by their signal victories of Medellin and Ciudad-Real. The operations of the army of Arragon had likewise been suspended by the necessity in which the French were, to recall to this province the body of troops under Marshal Mortier, and to place him at Valladolid, to carry succours to Marshal Ney, and re-establish the communications in Galicia.

Since the departure of the Emperor Napoleon and the commencement of the Austrian campaign, the French army in Spain had received no reinforcements to make up for its daily losses; instead of concentrating itself, it had continued, under King Joseph's orders, to be dispersed every day more and more over the Peninsula. Weak on every point, because we were too widely scattered, we exhausted ourselves by our very victories, and in Galicia, Portugal, and the Asturias, we had lost among the insurgent peasants that reputation of invincibility, more powerful still than the real force which had conquered so many nations.

King Joseph had been commander-in-chief since the departure of the Emperor. He fancied that he might attach the people of Spain to his sway after our arms had subdued them, by the well-known mildness of his character, in the same manner as he had gained the Neapolitans; and he had allowed the French troops to advance from all sides into the Peninsula, with the intention of organising provinces, that he might reign over a greater extent of country. It was thus that he compromised the military safety of the armies of Galicia and Portugal, which were five whole months without being heard of.

King Joseph had contracted habits of indolence upon the peaceful throne of Naples. Surrounded by flatterers, and by a few Spaniards who deceived him, he allowed himself to be misled by groundless hopes. Instead of following his armies, he remained in his capital, plunged in dissipation, and regretting the delights of Italy. He wanted to sleep and reign at Madrid, as he had done at Naples, even before we had conquered for him, supposing the conquest possible, a kingdom at the price of our blood.

He filled the columns of his state journals with decrees

which were never executed and scarcely read; he gave to one church the wax and sacred vases of another, pillaged long before by the French or stripped by the Spaniards themselves. He lavished the decorations of his royal order on his courtiers, who did not dare to wear them in any place that was not occupied by the French, for fear of being murdered by the Spanish peasants. King Joseph made several promotions in his army, which, however, was not as yet in existence; he gave away places in reversion, governments, administrations, and judgships in the most distant provinces in the kingdom in both hemispheres, while he dared not sleep even a few leagues from Madrid in one of his country houses. Like his brother at Paris, he pulled down old buildings to beautify his capital, but he had no money to raise a single new edifice, and the extent of his munificence was the removal of rubbish.

In order to please the people, he endeavoured by every possible means to imitate the solemn pomp, the grave ceremony, and even the tedious piety of his predecessors. He marched on foot at the head of processions through the streets of Madrid, making the officers of his staff and the soldiers of his bodyguard follow him with lighted tapers in their hands. All these pretensions to sanctity, his affectation of munificence, and his absurd prodigality, only made him an object of ridicule, when after the departure of Napoleon terror, which magnifies everything, had ceased.

The Spaniards had amused themselves with spreading a report that King Joseph was a one-eyed drunkard, which made a profound impression on the imagination of the country people. Nothing could be more untrue, but it was in vain that he endeavoured to overcome the popular prejudice by shewing himself often in public, and by looking full in the face of whosoever passed by; the people never lost the conceit that he was one-eyed.

On the day of his coronation the places of public

amusement were opened gratis, and at one of the theatres a farce, called Harlequin Emperor of the Moon, was played several times. During the representation, the people openly made applications to the ephemeral situation of King Joseph at Madrid. Devotees, who were accustomed to interlard all their conversation with the ejaculation, *Jesus, Maria, y Joseph*, stopped short when they had pronounced the two first names, and, pausing, would use the periphrase, *y el Padre de nuestro Senor*, lest they should draw down a benediction on King Joseph by naming the saint who was his supposed patron in heaven.

The very good nature of King Joseph came afterwards to be looked upon as weakness, even by the French themselves. After the great battles had been won, he would go himself to the prisoners sent from the army to the Retiro, and receive their oaths of fidelity, telling them that they had been deceived by traitors and that he, as their king, wished only for their happiness and that of their country. The prisoners, who expected nothing less than to be shot immediately, made no scruple of taking the oaths of submission required of them, but the moment they were armed and equipped they deserted and returned to their own armies, so that our soldiers called King Joseph the administrator and organiser-in-chief of the military depots of the Supreme Junta.

The French marshals and generals were very unwilling to obey a man whom they did not consider as a Frenchman, since he had been acknowledged king of Spain; and they often contradicted him, and sought to disgust him that they might be sent back into Germany. They would have been happy, at any price, to have quitted an irregular war, unpopular even in the army, and the more so as it deprived them of the opportunity of distinguishing themselves elsewhere and of obtaining high rewards by fighting under the emperor's own eye. This Spanish war was ruining France without even interesting the military honour of the nation.

King Joseph had neither enough of military talent and authority, nor sufficient confidence in himself to venture to command such operations as the changes in the general situation of affairs imperiously required. He dared not issue any new orders without consulting his brother; the plans sent from Paris or from Germany frequently arrived too late, and they could never be otherwise than imperfectly executed by one who had not conceived them; and the French troops in Spain wanted that unity in action, without which even the simplest operations of war cannot succeed.

In the month of April, Marshal Victor's corps, of which we formed a part, quitted the cantonment on the Guadiana between Merida and Medellin for a short time, and went to the neighbourhood of the Tagus and Alcantara, in order to join Lapisse's division. That corps had summoned Ciudad Rodrigo without effect. On the 14th May part of Marshal Victor's corps went again towards Alcantara, and crossed the river after a slight engagement with some of the Portuguese militia. The next day they reconnoitred in the direction of Castel Blanco, but learning that 8,000 English and Portuguese were in Abrantes, they conjectured that Marshal Soult's expedition against Lisbon had not succeeded, and consequently returned. Marshal Victor then collected his forces in the neighbourhood of Truxillo, between the Guadiana and the Tagus, to make sure of his communications by the bridge of Almarez, to cover Madrid, and to observe Cuesta's army. The fourth corps commanded by General Sebastiani remained in La Mancha after the affair of Ciudad Real.

On the 20th May the officers and subalterns of the fourth squadron of every cavalry regiment received orders from the war minister to repair to the general depots of their regiments in order to recruit. I quitted Spain in consequence of that order, and on my arrival in France I was sent against the

English on the coasts of Flanders. The expedition they had undertaken against the fleet and dockyards of Antwerp having failed in consequence of the slowness and indecision of their commander-in-chief, I returned to Spain in the beginning of the following year.

After Marshal Soult had been forced to abandon Oporto and to evacuate Portugal, the English army had re-crossed the Douro and occupied the towns of Thomar and Abrantes, near the Tagus, preparing to fall upon Spanish Estremadura by Coria and Placentia. Marshal Victor, whose corps occupied the neighbourhood of Truxillo and Caceres, fearing lest the English should get behind him along the right bank of the Tagus, crossed that river in the beginning of June and retired to Calzada, and afterwards on the 26th to Talavera de la Reyna.

On the 20th July, the English army under General Sir Arthur Wellesley joined Cuesta's Spanish army at Oropeza. The British force consisted of 20,000 English and 4,000 or 5,000 Portuguese; that of the Spanish General Cuesta amounted to 38,000 men. Another army of 18,000 or 20,000 Spaniards under the command of General Venegas, was preparing in La Mancha to co-operate with Generals Wellesley and Cuesta.

An advanced corps of Portuguese and Spaniards, commanded by the English General Wilson, went through the mountains towards Escalona, where it arrived on the 23rd, to communicate with General Venegas, whose force was advancing from Tembleque by Ocana, towards Aranjuez and Valdemoro. Generals Wilson and Venegas were to approach Madrid, and by the assistance of the inhabitants they hoped to get possession of it. The end of this combined movement appeared to be to force King Joseph to occupy himself about the safety of his capital, and to prevent him from concentrating his scattered forces. The Anglo-Spanish armies were in hopes of beating the French shortly, or at least, of driving them out of Madrid and the whole centre of Spain, and forcing them to cross the mountains and retire towards Segovia.

On the 22nd July, Generals Wellesley and Cuesta marched towards Talavera: Cuesta's cavalry gained a slight advantage, near the town, over the cavalry of the French rearguard, which instantly retired upon the main army. This success raised the hopes of the Spaniards to the highest pitch; eager to revenge their defeat at Medellin, by attacking the French, whom they fancied already half conquered, because they had fallen back, alone, they left the English at Talavera and imprudently advanced by El Bravo, and Santa Olalla to Torrijos.

Marshal Victor retired towards Toledo, behind the Guadarama, where he was joined on the 25th by General Sebastiani's corps and the troops brought by King Joseph from Madrid. The whole French army of the centre of Spain, being thus collected, amounted to 47,000 men. On the 26th it set out for Talavera under the command of King Joseph.

Nearly the whole of the dragoon regiment of Villa Viciosa was cut to pieces in the pass of Alcabon near Torrijos, by the 2nd Regiment of Hussars, which formed part of the French advanced guard, and the whole Spanish army retired precipitately behind the Alberche. The French army crossed that river the next day in the afternoon, drove in the English advanced posts, and arrived at about five o'clock in the evening within cannon shot of the enemy.

The Spanish army was placed in a position which it was not deemed possible to attack, behind old walls, and garden hedges which surround Talavera: the right was supported by the Tagus and the left by the right of the English, close to an unfinished redoubt on an eminence. The ground in front of the combined Anglo-Spanish army was unequal, and cut up in various parts by ravines formed by the winter rains; and the whole length of their position was covered by a pretty steep ravine, or bed of a torrent then dry. The left of the English was supported by a high round hillock, which commanded the greater part of the field of battle, and which was separated from the chains connected with the mountains of Castile by a pretty wide and deep valley.

The hillock might be called the key of the enemy's position, and against that point, a skilful general, gifted with that rapid power of perception which decides the fate of battles, would from the first have directed the greatest part of his means of attack, in order to get possession of it either by main force or by turning it by the valley: but the moment King Joseph was called upon to act, he was seized with a fatal spirit of hesitation and uncertainty. He tried half measures, disposed of the troops he had to command partially, and always lost, while he was groping, as it were, for time and opportunity to conquer. Marshal Jourdan was second in command, but in the war of Spain he was no longer animated by that spirit of patriotism which inspired him while he fought in the plains of Fleurus for the independence of France.

The French began by a cannonade straight forward from their right, accompanied by a fire from the rifle corps, and they sent a single battalion with some riflemen by the valley to gain the hillock by which the English left was supported, imagining that they were only thinking of retiring. This battalion, however, met with numerous troops, and was soon repulsed with loss and forced to fall back. A division of dragoons, which had been sent to reconnoitre towards Talavera, found all the avenues of the town strongly intrenched with artillery, and was prevented from advancing.

When night came, the French attempted anew to possess themselves of the hillock: a regiment of infantry, followed at some distance by two others, attacked the extremity of the English right with unequalled impetuosity, reached the summit of the hillock, and took possession, but it was soon forced to retire; having been fiercely attacked by a whole English division at the very moment when it was exhausted by the vigorous effort it had just made. One of the two regiments destined to support this attack had mistaken the direction through the woods in the dark, the other had been impeded on its march by the difficulty of finding the path in the ravine which covered the enemy's position.

These two successive attacks failed, notwithstanding the intrepidity and valour of the troops, because they were attempted by inefficient numbers; they had first sent a battalion and then a division, where a good part of the whole army ought to have gone. These fruitless attempts indicated to the English the projects of the French, for the next day, and made them doubly sensible of the importance and strength of the position they occupied, and which they spent the night in fortifying with artillery.

The sun rose on the following day on the two armies ranged in battle array, and the cannonade began anew: the action which was to ensue was probably to decide the fate of Portugal, which the English army had taken upon itself to defend, perhaps even that of the whole Peninsula might be affected by it. The old soldiers of the first and fourth corps of the French army, accustomed for years to conquest in every part of Europe, and to see their courage seconded by the able combinations of their leaders, waited with impatience for orders to engage, and depended on overthrowing all before them by a single well combined effort.

A division of three regiments of foot was sent by the valley, as it had been the day before, to assault the position, which for a moment we had in our power during the night. This division reached the height and was just preparing to take possession. One of the regiments advanced towards the enemy's artillery, when its charge was repulsed, and the whole division obliged to fall back. The English, judging by this new attack, that the French meant to turn their left by the valley, sent thither some of their cavalry, and placed a Spanish division on the declivities of the skirts of the Castilian mountains. The French returned to their first position, the cannonade continued for another hour, and then gradually ceased. The burning heat of the middle of the day forced the combatants on both sides to suspend the fight and to observe a sort of tacitly acknowledged truce, during which the wounded were carried off.

King Joseph, having at length reconnoitred the position of the enemy himself, ordered a general attack upon the English army at four o'clock in the afternoon. A division of dragoons was left near Talavera to observe the Spaniards. General Sebastiani's corps marched against the English right, while Marshal Victor's three divisions of infantry, followed by great bodies of cavalry, threw themselves upon their left in order to attack the hillock by way of the valley. King Joseph and Marshal Jourdan placed themselves with the reserve behind the fourth division; the cannon and musketry were soon heard.

The English commander-in-chief, placed on the height which commanded the whole field of battle, appeared at every point where danger required his presence. With a single glance he took in the various corps of his army, and distinguished below him the slightest movements of the French: he saw them form, dispose their columns for attack, judged of their projects by their dispositions, and thus had time to prevent and to baffle them by contrary arrangements. The position occupied by the English army, strong from situation and of difficult access both in front and on its flanks, was easily accessible on its rear, and permitted the troops to move with celerity towards any point which might be threatened.

98

The French had a ravine to cross before they could join their enemies; they had to advance over ground which was much cut up, muddy, and unequal, and which often forced them to break their line; they fought against positions fortified beforehand. The left, hidden by the rising ground, could not know what the right was doing; every division of the army fought with unequalled bravery, and even with skill, but there was no concert in their efforts; the French were not on that occasion moved and commanded by a general whose genius made up for the advantages which the nature of the ground might refuse to them, and give to their enemies.

Lapisse's division was the first to pass the ravine; it attacked the entrenched hillock, scaled it in spite of the grapeshot which thinned its ranks at every step, and was soon repulsed after having lost its general and many officers and soldiers; in retiring it left the right of the fourth division exposed, and it was taken in flank by the British artillery and forced for the moment to fall back. The left of General Sebastiani's corps had arrived, under a very brisk fire from the artillery, at the foot of the redoubt on the right of the English, the centre of the combined army. It had advanced too far and too soon, it was borne down and repulsed by the English right united with the Spanish left. That wing was, however, soon succoured and returned to the fight. In the centre Marshal Victor rallied Lapisse's division at the foot of the hillock, and gave up the attempt to gain it. The French then sought to turn it either by the right or left. Vilatte's division advanced into the valley, and Ruffin's, keeping on its right, followed the line at the foot of the Castilian mountains; the cavalry of the second line had prepared to over-run the plain as soon as the infantry should have forced a passage for them.

Two English regiments of cavalry then charged the French masses at the moment they put themselves in motion: the same regiments got into the valley and passed, regardless of the fire of several battalions of infantry, between Vilatte's and Ruffin's divisions, and fell with irresistible impetuosity on the 10th and 26th Regiments of French mounted chasseurs. The 10th could not stand the charge, it opened its ranks, but rallied soon afterwards, and the 23rd Light Dragoons which was at the head of the English cavalry was almost entirely destroyed or taken.

A division of the King of England's Guards, which formed the first line of the centre and left of the British army, having been charged, repulsed the French vigorously at first; but one of the brigades, having advanced too far, was in its turn taken in flank by the French artillery and infantry, and after suffering a severe loss, had some difficulty in retiring behind the second line. The French seized the momentary advantage and advanced again. One more effort only was required to gain the plain and fight the enemy on even ground, but King Joseph thought it too late to advance with the reserve, and the attack was put off till the next day. Night, however, came on, and the fight ceased from weariness without either party having gained sufficient advantage over the other to have any right to claim a victory.

Marshal Victor and Sebastiani's corps retired successively during the night upon the reserve, leaving an advanced post of cavalry upon the field of battle to carry off the wounded. The English, who expected a fresh attack the next morning, were much astonished, when daylight came, to see that their enemies had retired to their old position of the Alberche, and had abandoned twenty pieces of cannon. The French lost nearly 10,000 men; the English and Spaniards, according to their own accounts, 6,616.

King Joseph left the first division of the army upon the Alberche, and went with the fourth and the reserve to the assistance of Toledo; the garrison of that city consisted of only 1,500 men; it had been briskly attacked by a division of the Spaniards under General Venegas, who, on the 27th, had seized Aranjuez and Valdemoro.

A few days before, Madrid had been upon the point of being occupied by General Wilson's advanced posts which had advanced from Escalona, to Naval-Carnero. The inhabitants of the capital had opened their gates to him, and had come in crowds to meet him dressed in their holiday clothes, after having forced three French battalions who composed the garrison to shut themselves up in the fort of the Retiro. King Joseph threw a whole division into Toledo, and came on the 1st of August to Illescas, that he might be equally at hand to check the army of Venegas, to support the first division of his own army at Alberche, and to overawe the inhabitants of Madrid.

The English did not attempt to attack Marshal Victor; they retired on the 3rd August to Oropeza, leaving the Spaniards at Talavera, and General Wilson's corps at Escalona; and, in the night between the 4th and 5th, the combined English and Spanish armies precipitately re-crossed the Tagus by the bridge of Arzobispo, on the approach of the corps of Marshals Soult, Ney, and Mortier, who were advancing from Salamanca, by Puerto de Banos, Placentia, and Naval Moral, placing themselves between the English army and the bridge of Almaraz.

On the 8th August Marshal Mortier's advanced corps crossed the Tagus at a ford above the bridge of Arzobispo, at one o'clock in the afternoon, during the time of the siesta; it surprised a part of Cuesta's army, and seized his guns as well as those placed by the Spaniards to defend the bridge. On the 11th the army of Venegas was defeated at Almonacid in La Mancha by General Sebastiani. The Spanish and Portuguese troops of General Wilson were completely beaten on the 12th, among the mountains of Banos, by a part of Marshal Ney's force which was falling back on Salamanca.

The expedition of General Sir Arthur Wellesley into Estremadura was at least as hazardous as that attempted by General Moore against Marshal Soult at Saldanas, the year before. Had the corps of Marshals Soult, Ney, and Mortier arrived a single day sooner, the English and Spanish armies must have fallen into the power of the French: but King Joseph did not dare to dispose of these troops without first receiving the authority of the Emperor Napoleon. On the 22nd he had sent orders to Marshal Soult to concentrate the troops at Salamanca, and to march against the English army. The Marshal only received the orders on the 27th; he set off on the 28th, and notwithstanding all his expedition he did not arrive at Placentia till the 3rd August.

The English and Spanish forces remained behind the Tagus till the 20th August, occupying Messa de Ibor, Deleytosa, and Jaraicejo, opposite to Almaraz, where the bridge of boats had been destroyed by the Spaniards. They then fell back upon the Guadiana, and Sir Arthur Wellesley's troops returned into Portugal.

The invasion of Estremadura by the English forced the French to call up the three corps destined to guard and observe the provinces of the north of Spain, to the assistance of their central army, and from their union they had become very strong. After the departure of the English, the Spanish government still persisted in acting in large masses; an army of 55,000 men had been collected in La Mancha, and that army was completely beaten and dispersed at Ocana on the 10th November by Marshal Mortier with scarcely 24,000 men. It was not difficult for the French to defeat troops raised in haste, undisciplined, and ignorant of military manœuvres, in a pitched battle where the numbers which might have given them strength served only to embarrass them.

After the battle of Ocana the French ought to have collected their disposable troops anew, and to have marched directly upon Lisbon; but they passed the Sierra Morena, and without striking a blow they over-ran almost all Andalusia, excepting the isle of Leon and Cadiz. By extending themselves towards the south of Spain they gave the English time to fortify Portugal, and to form the military forces of that kingdom. The French became weak because they dispersed their troops, in order to occupy and organize a great extent of country; and the Spaniards seized the opportunity of carrying on that sort of national warfare, from which the French had suffered so much in the Asturias, Galicia, and the north of Portugal.

SECOND PART

V

AS THE Spanish armies had gradually been destroyed, the communications between the provincial juntas and the supreme central Junta had been cut off; each therefore, applied all its resources to the local defence of the district under its jurisdiction. Such of the inhabitants as had till then suffered with patience, daily expecting their deliverance after every pitched battle, now began to think of seeking from themselves individually the means of shaking off the yoke which oppressed them. Every province, every town, every individual felt more strongly every day the necessity of resisting the common enemy. The national hatred which existed against the French had produced a sort of unity in the undirected efforts of the people, and to regular warfare had succeeded a system of war in detail, a species of organised disorder which suited the fierce spirit of the Spanish nation exactly, as well as the unhappy circumstances in which it was placed.

That part of Spain occupied by the French was soon filled with partisans and guerrillas, some of them regular soldiers from the broken armies, and others the inhabitants both of mountain and valley: Clergy, husbandmen, students, shepherds even had become active and enterprising leaders. These leaders, without military authority, and without

104

permanent troops, were at first, as it were, only standards round which the inhabitants of the country rallied and fought. News of any little advantages gained by these numerous parties were eagerly received by the people and repeated with exaggeration, and they raised those hopes, which the defeat of their armies had for the moment depressed. That very liveliness of imagination and excessive spirit of independence, which had interfered with the slow and uncertain operations of the regular armies of the Junta, secured the continuance of the national war. And one might say of the Spaniards, that if at first they had been easily overcome, it was almost impossible to subdue them.

When we marched from one province to another, the partisans immediately reorganised the country we had abandoned in the name of Ferdinand VII, as if we were never to go back, and punished very severely everyone who had shewn any kind of zeal for the French. Thus the terror of our arms gave us no influence around us. As the enemy was spread over the whole country, the different points that the French occupied were all more or less threatened; their victorious troops, dispersed in order to maintain their conquests, found themselves in a state of continual blockade from Irun to Cadiz; and they were not in reality masters of more than the ground they actually trod upon.

The garrisons which they had left on the military roads to keep the country in check, were continually attacked. They were obliged to construct little citadels for their safety by repairing old ruined castles which they found on the heights, and these castles were frequently Roman or Moorish remains which, many centuries before, had served the same purpose. In the plains, the posts of communication fortified one or two of the houses at the entrance of each village for safety during the night, or as a place of retreat when attacked. The sentinels dared not remain without the fortified enclosures for fear of being carried off; they therefore stationed themselves on a tower, or on a wooden scaffolding built on the roof near the chimney to observe what passed in the surrounding country.

The French soldiers thus shut up in their little fortresses frequently heard the gay sounds of the guitars of their enemies, who came to pass their nights in the neighbouring villages, where they were always well received and feasted by the inhabitants. The French armies could only obtain provisions and ammunition under convoy of very strong detachments, which were for ever harassed and frequently intercepted. These detachments met with but slight resistance in the plains, but the moment they approached the mountains, they were obliged to cut their way forward by force of arms; and the daily losses of the French, in many parts of Spain, in their attempts to procure victuals, and to keep up their communications, were at least equal to any they could have sustained if they had had to struggle with an enemy who could have met them in open battle.

The people of Spain did not allow themselves to be cast down by the length of the war. In some provinces the peasants were always armed; the husbandman guided his plough with one hand, while he held in the other a sword always unsheathed, and which was only buried on the approach of the French if they were too numerous to be fought. Their animosity increased by the vexations which the French made them suffer. The evils to which other nations submit because they look on them as the inevitable consequences of war, only furnished the Spaniards with new subjects for hatred and irritation. In order to satiate their inveterate resentment, they employed by turns the greatest energy or the deepest dissimulation and cunning where they were the weakest. Like avenging vultures eager for prey, they followed the French columns at a distance to murder such of the soldiers as, fatigued or wounded, remained behind on a march.

Sometimes they invited the French to a feast on their arrival, and would endeavour to intoxicate the soldiers that they might plunge them into that security which is an hundred times more dangerous than all the chances of battle. They then called upon the partisans, and indicated, during the night, the houses in which their enemies had imprudently trusted themselves. When new Frenchmen sought to revenge the death of their comrades the inhabitants fled, and they found nothing in the villages but deserted dwellings, on which they could only wreak vengeance at their own expense, for they could not destroy a house, even an empty one, without cutting off their own resources for the future.

When our detachments arrived in any force at the insurgent towns of Biscay or Navarre, the *alcades*, with the women and children, came out to meet us, as if all had been at peace, and no noise was heard but that of the smiths' hammers; but at the moment of our departure all labour ceased, and the inhabitants seized their arms to harass our detachments among the rocks, and to attack our rearguards. This sort of warfare, where there was no fixed object upon which the imagination could dwell, damped the ardour of the soldier, and wore out his patience.

The French could only maintain themselves in Spain by terror; they were constantly under the necessity of punishing the innocent with the guilty, and of taking revenge on the weak for the offences of the powerful. Plunder had become necessary for existence, and such atrocities as were occasioned by the enmity of the people, and the injustice of the cause for which the French were fighting, injured the moral feeling of the army, and sapped the very foundations of military discipline, without which regular troops have neither strength nor power.

Towards the end of the year 1809 I returned to Spain, with a reinforcement of eighty hussars, to my regiment. In the interior of France it was believed, according to the gazettes, that the English, who had retreated to Portugal after the battle of Talavera, were only waiting for the first fair wind to take them home; that the conquered country had long been quietly subjected to King Joseph, and that the French armies, safe in good cantonments, had now nothing to do but to destroy a few banditti, who plundered the peaceable inhabitants, and laid them under contribution.

At Bayonne we joined several other detachments of light horse, and we crossed the Bidassoa in order to sleep at Irun. A great number of the inhabitants of all ages had assembled at the gates of that town to see us enter, and then followed us with evident curiosity for some time. We thought, at first, that this mark of attention was intended to show that they were glad to see us in their country, but we afterwards learned that the inhabitants of Irun, as well as those of other frontier towns, kept an exact account of all the French who entered Spain, as well as of the wounded who quitted it, and that it was according to these reports that the partisans and guerrillas directed their operations.

All the detachments which, like us, were going to reinforce the divers corps of the army of Spain, received orders to assemble in the towns of Miranda and Vittoria, to be in readiness for an expedition against the Spanish partisans of Navarre and La Rioca. General Simon set out from Vittoria on the 23rd December, with 1,200 men, to occupy Salvatierra and Allegria. The commandants of the garrisons left in the towns of Navarre had formed moveable columns, and they were to join General Simon's corps after having dispersed such parties as they might meet on their march. The intention of this kind of military chase was to destroy Mina's guerrilla bands, which held Pampeluna in a state of almost perpetual blockade, and were continually attacking the detachments and convoys on their way to the French army in Arragon.

Generals Loison and Solignac marched from Vittoria and Miranda on the 16th, and threw themselves at once by both banks of the Ebro upon Logronio, in hopes of surprising the Marquis de Porliere in that city. The numerous guerrillas of that chief intercepted our communications between Bayonne and Madrid, and made incursions almost daily even to the gates of Burgos, Bribiesca, Pancorvo, Miranda, and Vittoria. My detachment of hussars formed part of a corps of four or five thousand men, commanded by General Loison. The foot soldiers had left their baggage and even their knapsacks behind them, that they might be light for running in the mountains.

At four o'clock in the afternoon of the 17th we came in sight of Logronio. General Solignac's troops arrived before the town at the same time; they immediately took possession of all the gates and outlets on the right bank of the Ebro, while we seized the bridge leading to the left of that river. We flattered ourselves for a moment that we had surrounded the partisans in Logronio, but, to our great astonishment, we soon afterwards entered the town without having to fire a single gun.

The Marquis Porliere had been warned of our combined march early in the morning, and had made his escape, by cross roads, to the high mountains of Castile. The inhabitants of the town, men and women, appeared at the windows to see us come in; and an air of satisfaction and content shone generally on their countenances, but it was satisfaction at the escape of the Marquis Porliere and certainly not at the arrival of the French, who, they well knew by experience, were come to exact the arrears of their contributions.

The next day General Solignac set out in pursuit of the enemy; at Najera he met a small Spanish party which he pursued as far as La Calzada di San Domingo, fancying that he was to come up with the main body of the guerrillas; but it was a stratagem of the Marquis Porliere to draw us on in an opposite direction to that which he had taken with his little army. General Loison followed General Solignac to Najera on the 19th, where we were forced to remain two whole days in order to obtain information concerning the enemy, all traces of whom we had entirely lost.

At length on the 21st we learned that the Marquis Porliere had taken the road towards Soto; that town, situated among the mountains, was the residence of a provincial junta, and contained magazines of arms, ammunition, and clothing. We set out again in pursuit of the partisans going up the Najerillo. General Loison's division went to pass a few hours of the night in a village situated at the foot of the high mountains ten leagues south of Soto. A detached corps composed of my party of hussars, a hundred and fifty Polish lancers, and two hundred voltigeurs, continued to pursue the enemy. I cleared the way with an advanced guard of twenty-five hussars. We went through narrow and difficult roads, through deep snows, and at sunrise we reached the enemy's rearguard, from which we took a few prisoners. We stopped several hours to feed our horses, and to give General Loison time to come up with us. At noon we set off again, on the left bank of a little river which runs down towards Soto.

On the summits of the highest mountains on our right we saw peasants making their escape with their cattle, and small parties of Spanish horsemen, acting as watches on the heights, successively galloped off as soon as they perceived us. The clergy and *alcades* of the villages we had to go through, with feigned zeal, brought us refreshments in order to delay our march. Of fifty or sixty peasants of different ages, of whom I made inquiries in different places, there was not one who did not endeavour to deceive us by saying that they had seen none of their partisans, and that they were not at Soto. Nevertheless, horses dying of fatigue,

110

abandoned on the roads with their furniture, proved to us almost at every step that we were approaching the enemy.

When we came within about a quarter of a league of Soto, we were received by a discharge of thirty or forty muskets, and we saw some armed peasants suddenly appear from behind the rocks, where they had lain in ambush, and run down the hill towards Soto as fast as they were able. We halted to wait for the infantry and our major commandant. There was no room to form in line on the height, so we remained in file in the narrow path by which we had come up the hill.

Soto is situated at the bottom of a narrow valley crossed by a torrent; beyond the town is a very steep mountain, on the side of which a winding road has been made. It was by that road that we saw the partisans retreat before our faces. The magistrates of the junta of Soto, and a number of priests in long black cloaks, marched first; they were near the summit of the mountain; they were followed by the treasure and baggage upon mules tied behind one another in files; then came the soldiers in uniform, and a number of peasants armed with fowling pieces, marching without any order, and a crowd of inhabitants of all ages and sexes, hastening out of the town pell mell with the guerrillas. The agitation of so great a number of men pressing by different paths towards the tops of the heights offered the most picturesque appearance to the eye.

Disorder took place among the Spaniards the moment they saw us, and they at first quickened their march, but seeing afterwards that we formed only a scanty outpost they recovered, and the whole side of the mountain echoed with long guttural shouts. Those who were nearest to us stopped, and placed themselves in the rocks, whence they pointed their guns at us from every side, and we heard these words, mixed with a thousand curses, 'Come, if you dare, and look at the *robbers* a little closer.' It was by this name that our

111

soldiers called them on account of their manner of fighting in disorder. They were separated from us by a ravine three or four hundred feet deep, at the bottom of which was the river.

To cover his retreat the Marquis Porliere had left a company of cavalry before the gate by which we had to enter Soto, and at a little distance on the other side of the river he had placed four or five hundred infantry on the rocks and terraces which commanded the town. Whatever happened, these men had it in their power to retire at our approach without running the smallest risk, after having done us a great deal of mischief.

The major of the 26th Regiment of the Line, who commanded us, judged that the position of the enemy was not assailable in front, and he therefore resolved to turn it. A hundred and fifty of our riflemen went down into the ravine and forded the river below us; they then, with much difficulty, climbed the opposite mountain, and fired at the enemy for some time without gaining ground. Their ammunition being nearly exhausted, they retired round a little chapel on the top of the mountain, and sent two men to inform us of their situation. The shouts, the curses, and the fire of the Spaniards then redoubled; they had seen our riflemen send for assistance, and also that we could not afford them any.

The captain of the enemy's cavalry advanced about half a musket shot before the troop he commanded, near the entrance of the town, and tried by abuse to provoke the officer who commanded the advanced party of the French hussars. He curvetted his horse, and flourished his sabre to shew he knew the use of it. The hussar officer looked at him at first with tolerable coolness; but, out of patience at last with the bravadoes and shouts of the Spaniards who were opposite, and whose boldness was increasing, he went down the narrow and abrupt path leading to Soto alone. The enemy's captain turned his horse when he came within a few paces of him, and quietly returned to his own party.

Meantime the uneasiness of the major of the 26th increased every moment. General Loison did not make his appearance; day was closing in; no more firing was heard from the opposite mountain; and we had no farther tidings of our riflemen.

When night came, we heard the Spanish drum beat a kind of rally, and shortly after we saw a pretty brisk fire of musketry beyond the valley, between two parties disputing the passage of the river. A deep silence succeeded to the noise of the fire.

Night and loneliness augmented our uncertainty. We fancied that our riflemen had come down from the mountain to force their way through the enemy and join us, and we feared lest, being overpowered by numbers, they might be in imminent danger; our major commandant sent my detachment to their assistance. On entering the town, instead of the Spaniards we met General Loison's division filing in: that corps, misled by their guides, had taken a very long road, completely different from that we had followed. The engagement which had appeared so bloody to us from a distance had taken place between our riflemen and the grenadiers of General Loison's advanced guard; their friendly troops arriving at the same time in opposite directions, fortunately recognised each other after the second volley. The darkness had prevented them from taking aim, and they lost but one man between them.

The town of Soto had been deserted by its inhabitants; it soon resounded with the hollow shouts of the soldiers as they ran about the narrow streets, breaking open the doors to procure provisions and lodging. In the midst of these confused sounds, which were infinitely multiplied by the mountain echoes, were heard the cries of a woman in delirium, who with a more than human voice called for help during the whole night. She had been left in the hospital of the town when the inhabitants departed, and had been forcibly struck with the commotion which was new to her, and which she saw through the grated windows of the room in which she was shut up. That voice raised in the midst of the tumult seemed like the organ of the whole population which had fled from the town.

A fire shortly broke out on the height; we heard walls falling with a great crash, and soon after there was an explosion, and we saw the flaming beams of a building thrown up into the air. Some cases of cartridges which the enemy had concealed among some straw, because they could not carry them off, had exploded.

We quitted Soto at sunrise, and for two days and a night we continued to follow the track of the guerrillas towards Munilla and Cervera. Despairing at length of coming up with them to give them battle, we took up quarters at the small town of Arnedo, and afterwards returned to Logronio.

General Simon succeeded no better in his expedition into Navarre against Mina; that chief, attacked on the 19th at Estella and the 20th at Puenta de la Reyna, disbanded his force, and thus escaped the troops that were marching against him from all quarters. Mina re-assembled his bands immediately after the departure of General Simon. The Marquis Porliere, driven from the mountains of Castile, returned afterwards and stationed himself in those of Asturia. He had not lost thirty men in his retreat, during which he had been pursued by troops at least four times more numerous than those he commanded.

We see by the reports of the French commanders, that bands similar to those of Porliere and Mina existed in all the other provinces of Spain occupied by the French. These bands did incalculable mischief to our troops, and it was impossible to destroy them. Always pursued and often dispersed, they rallied and recommenced their incursions immediately.

We remained nearly a month in the province of La Rioca, while General Loison was collecting the arrears of the contributions, and we afterwards went towards Burgos, in order to join our regiment in Andalusia. We arrived at Madrid on the 25th January, and we remained five days in a village near that capital, to wait for a detachment of our regiment which was coming direct from France with baggage, money, and a number of fresh horses. This new detachment having joined us, an adjutant, to whose care it had been trusted, took the command of our column of hussars; we crossed La Mancha and soon arrived at Santa-Cruz, a small town situated at the foot of the Sierra Morena. These mountains, which separate La Mancha from Andalusia, are inhabited by some colonists brought by Count Olivades from different parts of Germany in 1781. The oldest of those colonists followed us on foot for whole hours to enjoy, for the last time before their death, the happiness of speaking their native tongue with such of our hussars as were their countrymen.

The moment one passes the mountains one enters Andalusia. The difference of heat in the atmosphere is instantly perceptible, and the magnificence of the landscape that presents itself forms a striking contrast with the sterility of the Black Mountains, or Sierra Morena, one leaves behind. The husbandmen were occupied in gathering the olives, and the country presented, towards the end of winter, that smiling and animated appearance which is only seen in more northern climates at vintage or at harvest time.

On our left were the mountains of the kingdom of Jaen, and in the distance the snowy summits of the Sierra Nevada of Grenada, reared their perpetually white tops, the last retreats of the Moors before their final expulsion from Spain.

The road lay between long plantations of olives, under whose protecting shade vines and corn were alternately springing. The fields are surrounded by hedges of aloes whose leaves are as pointed as lances, and whose straight slender stems shoot up to the height of trees. Here and there we saw tufted orchards planted with orange trees behind the dwelling houses, and on the waste lands on the banks of the rivulets, the white laurel and the oleander were then in flower. A few old palm trees are still seen here and there in the gardens of the clergy, who preserve them for the sake of distributing the branches on Palm Sunday.

We marched upon both banks of the Guadalquivir, following the different turns of that river between Andujar and Cordova. The country is less picturesque on approaching Seville. We crossed plains of corn of several leagues in extent, without seeing either habitations or trees, and there are extensive tracts left waste which furnish pasture for immense flocks of sheep.

Andalusia is undoubtedly by nature the most fertile and opulent part of Spain. There is a proverb current in the Castiles and La Mancha, that *'the water of the Guadalquivir fattens more horses than the barley of other countries.'* The bread of Andalusia is considered as the whitest and most exquisite in the world, and the olives are of most extraordinary size. The air is so serene and pure, that one may sleep in it during the greater part of the year; and one frequently sees men lying all night in the verandas in summer, and sometimes even in winter. A number of individuals who are not very rich, travel without troubling themselves to seek a nightly lodging; they carry their provisions with them, or buy such food as is prepared by women on stoves at the gates or in the great squares of large cities, for passengers. The poor never ask each other whether they have a house to lie in, as in other countries, but they inquire if they have a cloak sufficient to preserve them from the immediate influence of the sun's rays in summer, and to throw off the winter rains.

116

In Andalusia, still more than in any other province in the Peninsula, one meets with traces and monuments of the Arabs at every step; and it is the singular mixture of the customs and usages of the east, with Christian manners, which distinguishes the Spaniards from the other nations of Europe.

The town houses are almost all built on the Moresco plan; in the middle they have a large court paved with flag stones, in the centre of which there is a basin, whence fountains continually rise and refresh the air; the basin is shaded by the cypress and the lemon tree. Trelice work, supporting orange trees, whose leaves, flowers, and fruit last all the year, frequently covers the walls. The different apartments communicate with each other by the court, and there is commonly an interior gate on the same side with the door opening to the street.

In the ancient palaces of the Moorish kings and nobles, such as the Alhambra of Grenada, the courts are surrounded with colonades or porticos, whose narrow and numerous arches are supported by very tall slender columns; ordinary houses have a single and very plain interior court, with a cistern shaded by a large citron tree in one corner. A sort of pitcher or jar,* in which water is put to cool, usually hangs near the door or wherever there is a current of air. These pitchers are called *alcarazas*, and their name, which is Arabic, indicates that they were brought into Spain by the Moors.

There is one of these open courts within the walls of the cathedral of Cordova, which was an ancient mosque. This court, like those of private houses, is shaded by citrons and

---

*These jars have the same form, and are applied to the same purposes, as those described by M. Denon, in his travels in Egypt; and which are made on the banks of the Nile, between Tentyre, Kenah, and Thebes.

cypresses, and contains basins in which the water is kept continually pure and full by fountains. On entering the consecrated part of the *Mezquita*, for the temple has preserved its antique appellation even to our days, one is struck with astonishment at the sight of a multiplicity of columns of different coloured marbles. These columns are ranged in parallel lines pretty near each other, and they support a sort of open arcade covered with a wooden roof. This multitude of columns crowned with arcades, reminds one of a forest of palm trees, whose branches, regularly trained round, touch each other as they bend.

The chapel where the book of the laws was kept, is now under the guardianship of Saint Peter. A high altar for performing mass, and a choir where canons chaunt the service, have been placed in the middle of that Mussulman mosque, and have converted it in our days into a Christian temple. These coincidences are continually met with in Spain, and recall to mind the triumph of Christianity over Mahomedanism.

The Andalusians bring up numerous flocks, which they feed in the plains during winter, and send in summer to graze on the tops of the mountains. The yearly and customary transmigration of large flocks at fixed times, originates in Arabia, where the practice is very ancient.

The Andalusian horses are descended from the generous breed brought over in former times by the Arabs, and the same distinctions paid in Arabia to pure and noble blood in these animals are also still regarded in Spain. The Andalusian horse is proud, spirited, and gentle; the sound of the trumpet pleases and animates him; and the noise and smoke of powder do not frighten him. He is sensible of caresses, and docile to the voice of his master: so when he is overcome with fatigue, his master, instead of beating him, flatters and encourages him. The horse then seems to recover his strength, and sometimes does from mere emulation what blows could never have extorted from him.

We were often followed by Spanish peasants, who led the baggage, victuals and ammunition upon their own horses and mules. One day I heard one of them after a long speech to his horse, who could scarcely walk, whisper closely in his ear with great eagerness, and as if he wished to spare him an affront in the eyes of his fellows, 'Take care that nobody sees you.' At the same moment a child was saying to his ass, 'Curse the mother who bred thee.' Asses are treated much worse than horses, for they are not supposed capable of the same feelings of honour.

People commonly travel on horseback in Spain, and the carriage of goods is in many provinces still on the backs of mules. The fine roads which cross Spain are very modern. The streets of the old towns are narrow and winding, and the stories of the houses jut out farther the higher they are. These streets of Moorish building are not made for carriages. Excepting a few hotels founded by Italians in the large cities, the inns of Andalusia, and indeed of all Spain, are large caravanseras where one finds nothing but lodging, and room for horses and mules. Travellers are obliged to carry provisions with them, and to sleep upon their horse-cloths. The natives of the country travel in small caravans whenever they go off the most public roads, and they carry guns slung to their saddle bows for fear of being robbed by the smugglers, who are very numerous in the mountains of Grenada and on the southern coasts between Malaga and Cadiz. In some parts of Spain, the country people and particularly the farm servants sleep stretched out upon mats which they roll up and carry about with them. This eastern custom explains the words of our Saviour, 'Take up thy bed and walk.'

The country women sit, in the Moorish manner, on circular mats of reeds, and in some convents of Spain, where the ancient manners are transmitted without alteration, the

119

nuns still sit like Turks, without knowing that they derive the custom from the enemies of the Christian faith. The mantilla, a sort of large woollen veil commonly worn by the lower class of women in Andalusia and which sometimes hides their whole face except their eyes, seems to have originated in the large scarf in which the eastern women wrap themselves when they go out. The Spanish dances, particularly the different kinds of fandango, resemble the loose dances of the east. The custom of playing the castanets in dancing, and of singing seguedillas, still exists among the Arabs of Egypt as well as in Spain, and the burning wind which blows from the east still receives the name of the Medina wind in Andalusia.

Like the Orientals, the Spanish in general are sober, even in the midst of abundance, from a religious principle; they look upon intemperance as an abuse of the gifts of God, and entertain a profound contempt for those who give themselves up to it. They eat salt pork every day at their meals; this meat, unwholesome in hot countries, is prohibited by the sacred laws of all the nations of the east and is an abomination to them. At the time when Spain was conquered by the Christians, and before the entire expulsion of the Moors, there were in Andalusia a great number of Mussulmans and Jews, who had become converts in appearance only in order to obtain permission to remain in the country. The Christian Spaniards then eat pork, as a test among themselves, and it was, so to speak, a kind of profession of faith.

There is, even in our days, so striking an analogy between the mode of warfare in many parts of Spain, and that of various tribes whom the French had to fight on the banks of the Nile, that, if we were to substitute Spanish for Arab names in many pages of the history of the campaign in Egypt, it might pass for the description of the events of the Spanish war.

The Spanish national and local troops, or the levies in mass, fight in disorder and with loud shouts. In an attack in the open country they have that impetuosity, that fury mingled with despair and fanaticism which distinguishes the Arabs, and like them they are apt to despair too soon of the event and yield the battle at the very moment they might claim the victory; but when they fight behind walls and entrenchments their firmness is unconquerable. The inhabitants of Egypt fled into the defiles of the mountains beyond the desert. The inhabitants of Spain quitted their dwellings on the approach of our troops, and carried their most precious effects into the mountains. In Spain as in Egypt our soldiers could not remain behind their companies without being murdered. In short, the inhabitants of the south of Spain possess the same perseverance in hatred, and the same liveliness of imagination which distinguish the nations of the east. Like them, they are easily discouraged on the least rumour of defeat, and rise up in arms the moment they conceive the slightest hopes of success. The Spaniards, like the Arabs, often treated their prisoners with the excess of barbarity, but they also sometimes exercised towards them the noblest and most generous hospitality.

VI

AFTER having passed Andujar, Cordova, Epica, and Carmona, we reached Seville, where we received orders from Marshal Soult to join our regiment at Ronda, a town situated about ten leagues from Gibraltar. We were at first struck with the profound tranquillity which reigned over the plains of Andalusia; the greater number of the large towns had sent deputations to King Joseph; but the tranquillity was but apparent and only existed in such parts as were filled with numerous French troops. The inhabitants of the kingdoms of Murcia and Grenada, the province of Ronda, with all those of the mountains which intersect or surround Andalusia, as well as those which separate it from Estremadura and Portugal, had taken arms simultaneously.

We quitted Seville on the 18th March, and slept at Outrera, and on the 19th we went on to Moron, a small town situated at the foot of the mountains of Ronda; the inhabitants of the town were on the point of joining their neighbours in the mountains, who had long been in a state of general insurrection. The greatest part of the population of Moron assembled in the principal square the moment we arrived. The men looked at us with an expression of constrained fury and appeared to watch our least motions, not to satisfy curiosity, but to accustom themselves to the sight of enemies whom they proposed shortly to fight, and thus to get rid of that fear of what is unknown which acts so powerfully on a people of lively imagination. Some of the women were dressed in English stuffs on which the pictures of Ferdinand VII and the Spanish generals most distinguished in the war against the French were painted.

When we perceived the fermentation and spirit of revolt which existed in the town we determined on taking up our lodgings close together in three neighbouring inns. If we had dispersed to lodge in the different houses of the inhabitants, as we might safely have done in the plains, we should, probably, all have been murdered in the night.

We had but very few men in a state to fight, because we had a number of spare horses to lead, and besides we escorted the military chest of the regiment and various equipments, which were conveyed upon mules and asses furnished by requisition, so that our march was slow and difficult. A quartermaster and I were the only persons of the detachment who had ever been in Spain before, or who could speak the language. The quartermaster remained with our commanding adjutant as interpreter, and I always preceded the body of the troop by a few hours to procure provisions and lodgings wherever we had to halt.

On leaving Moron we entered the mountains of Ronda to proceed to Olbera. I set off as usual a little before the detachment to prepare quarters, accompanied by a hussar and a young trooper who had been picked out from the recruits for a scout. At two leagues from Moron I knocked at the door of a farmhouse on the mountain; an elderly man tremblingly opened it, and I asked for something to drink, which he gave me with extraordinary zeal. I afterwards learned that there was a little band of five armed smugglers in the house who were afraid of being discovered.

The advanced guard coming up with us soon afterwards,

I was afraid I should not have time to prepare provisions and quarters before the arrival of the detachment. We could only proceed very slowly because the road was hilly and difficult, and our horses had been continually on the march for several months. I gave mine to the hussar to lead, and mounted that of a guide whom we had taken at Moron. I set off before my companions and arrived alone within sight of Olbera. A deep valley, bare of trees, into which the road descends abruptly, separated me from the town, which is placed among rocks on the summit of a high hill which commands the whole country.

As I advanced, the peasants, who were at work in the neighbouring fields in bands of eight or ten together, according to the custom of the country, became inquisitive concerning the cause of my coming and quitted their labours immediately to follow me down the path. The inhabitants of the village had long perceived me and they came out in crowds upon the rocks to watch me. I began to fear lest there should be no French in Olbera, as I had at first imagined, and I stopped at the bottom of the valley surprised at the increasing agitation I perceived. I hesitated a moment whether I should turn back, but I thought it best to go on at any risk. The horse I rode was tired with the journey he had come, and the road I must have gone over again was very steep; I was besides closely followed by a troop of peasants armed with mattocks.

They soon reached and surrounded me, and asked what province I came from, and what news I brought. I saw immediately by their gestures that they thought I was in the Spanish service. My dark brown uniform was the cause of their mistake, and I took care not to undeceive them, not being sure whether I could do so without risking my life. I hoped to gain time till the arrival of my friends, and let the peasants think that I was a Swiss officer in the service of the Junta, and that I was on my way to Gibraltar. I added, to

124

put them in good humour, that the Marquis de la Romana had just gained a great victory near Badajos. The peasants received this news with eagerness, and as they repeated it to each other they loaded the French with a thousand imprecations which gave me but a melancholy notion of the fate which awaited me if by any chance I was discovered.

In return for my communication I asked those who surrounded me, if their village contained any of those hateful Frenchmen? They said that King Joseph, with his guards, had been repulsed from Gaucin, that they had quitted Ronda some days before, and that that town must by that time be occupied by 10,000 mountaineers. It was at Ronda that we were to join our regiment. If it really was in the hands of the enemy, our detachment had nothing to expect but entire destruction in the mountains. The peasants stopped to drink at a spring on the road and I continued to climb the hill alone.

I soon saw five men armed and equipped as soldiers, hastening on to get before me by a cross road, and they entered Olbera before I reached it. Hearing loud shouting, I had no doubt but that the five men had brought the news of the approach of our detachment and that they had discovered that I was a Frenchman. I stopped once more, doubting whether I should go on. The inhabitants, who were watching me from the rocks, saw my hesitation and their shouts increased. A number of women had stationed themselves on a height which overlooked the entrance of the village, and their shrill voices, mingled with the tones of the men, sounded like the wind whistling in a storm. I determined on advancing, and I believe I should have been lost if I had then attempted to go back. I should have seemed to acknowledge myself in the wrong, which an enraged multitude seldom forgives.

I soon saw a *corregidor*, and *alcade*, and two priests approach me, preceded by five or six persons, at the head of whom was a young man who, as I afterwards discovered, was the *gracioso* of the village. He said to me in Spanish, with an air of mockery, 'Certainly the ladies of Olbera will receive you well, they are very fond of the French;' and, sneeringly, made many other similar jests.

One of his companions in a strong voice asked me how many Frenchmen were following me. I told him there were two hundred, more or less. He answered rudely enough, ''Tis false, there are not a hundred, counting yourself. The five men who are just come to the village saw them from the farm-house on the road from Moron.'

I saw clearly that they knew who I was. The priests and the *corregidor* having now approached, I thought, from their portentous faces, that they were going to propose to administer extreme unction. Amidst the tumult of voices I heard the following words distinctly articulated, 'You must hang him, he is a Frenchman, he is the devil himself, he is the devil incarnate.'

The noise suddenly ceased to my great astonishment, and I saw the Spaniards disperse; the trooper, the hussar, and the guide whom I had left behind had just appeared on the opposite height, and those who had been stationed to watch on the highest rocks took them at a distance for the advanced guard of our detachment, and immediately by shouts and gestures gave notice to the mob which surrounded me.

The *corregidor* and the *alcade* soon changed their tone, and told me, bowing very low, that they were the magistrates of the place, that they paid me their respects in consequence of the decree of King Joseph, which ordered all constituted authorities in Spain to go out and meet the French troops and to receive them well. My confidence increasing with the civility shewn me by the magistrates and with the fear they began to shew, I advised them, with some threats, to keep the people quiet and ordered them to prepare victuals for the troops which were coming up.

To excuse, in some manner, what had happened, the *corregidor* begged me not to attach any importance to the shouts of a few drunkards, who amused themselves by stirring up the people; and when I questioned them concerning the five armed men who had entered the village a few moments before, one of the priests, with an insinuating voice, told me rather ironically that they were shooting small birds, and that the bags they had over their shoulders were full of game, and I was obliged to be satisfied with such excuses, however bad. I got off my horse and walked with the priests and *alcades* to the town house, which was in the great square, at the top of the village, and we began to make out billets for the soldiers' quarters.

The trooper, who was of my party, left the hussar with my horse at the entrance of the village and galloped straight up to the house where I was. He had hardly alighted when the Spaniards crowded from the neighbouring streets with terrible shouts. They expected a large body of troops, but when they saw a single man ride through their village, they recovered from their error, and ran furiously out of their houses. Their rage was such that they crushed one another in an arched way which leads to the great square.

I immediately went out to the balcony, and called my trooper to come up, which he did, and we shut and barricadoed ourselves into the council room. The people stopped a moment to seize the trooper's horse, portmanteau and pistols; the ringleaders of the riot then seized the staircase and got to the door of the room where we had just shut ourselves up, with the *corregidor* and the two priests, and they called out to us through the partition to surrender.

I made the *corregidor*, whom I kept in my hands, order them to be quiet and told them that our detachment was coming immediately, that we should sell our lives dearly, and that if they attempted to come in, their own father priest should be the first victim of their fury. Being afraid they would force the door, I went back as far as the narrowest entrance of a second chamber, holding the priest by the arm that I might use him as a shield in case of need. I drew my sword and ordered the trooper to do the same, and to remain at the end of the room, in order to prevent the vicar and the *corregidor* from seizing me by the shoulders. The shouts of the people were soon renewed, and those of the inhabitants who had just been conferring with us, were pushed back again by a new crowd on the staircase and in the square. The door was several times violently shaken, and seemed on the point of yielding to the efforts of the assailing mob.

I then said to the priest, 'Pardon me, reverend father; you see that I cannot resist the populace. I am forced by necessity to make you a partaker of my fate, and we shall soon die together.'

The vicar, frightened at the danger of the priest, and also at that which threatened himself, went out upon the balcony, and cried aloud to the inhabitants that their chief priest would infallibly perish if they did not instantly retire. The women screamed at these words, and the mob unanimously and instantly fell back, so deep and so real is the veneration of the Spanish people for their priests.

The trooper and I kept up this sort of blockade for some time longer. The square soon ceased to echo with the reiterated clamours of the enraged people, and the trampling of the horses of my friends who were forming in line at the lower end of the village came to my ear as distinctly at noon as if it had been in the silence of deep midnight.

We joined the detachment along with the *corregidor* and the priest whom we kept with us as a safeguard. I told my comrades what had happened, and advised them to go, on the same day, to Ronda, after feeding our horses.

Notwithstanding all my representations, the adjutant who commanded us insisted on passing the night at Olbera, saying, as a kind of reproach, that it was a thing unheard of, that troops of the line should derange themselves for peasants. The adjutant had just passed several years in France, at the depot of the regiment, and had not yet learned to know the Spaniards.

We formed a bivouac in a meadow surrounded by walls belonging to an inn upon the road at the bottom of the village. During the remainder of the day the inhabitants were apparently quiet enough and furnished us with provisions; but, instead of a young ox which I had asked for, they brought us an ass cut up in quarters. The hussars thought the veal, as they called it, tasted very flat, but it was not till long afterwards that we learned from the mountaineers themselves the whimsical trick that had been put upon us. After that, they often used to cry out, as they fired upon us, 'Who eat asses' flesh at Olbera!' – the greatest affront, in their opinion, that could be offered to Christians.

Not daring to attack us in the enclosure in which we were entrenched, they prepared for the moment of our departure, and gave notice to the inhabitants of the different towns and villages in the neighbourhood to place ambuscades and expect us the next day on the road to Ronda. Towards night they assumed a threatening attitude; they posted themselves in great numbers on the rocks and formed a kind of close hedge around the entrance of our bivouac. There they remained immovable, watching our slightest motions. A few voices, quickly suppressed by the *alcades*, broke upon the silence from time to time, in order to insult our sentinels.

Rather late at night, the priest presented himself at the bivouac begging to speak to me. He told me that he had prepared excellent lodgings for the officers of our troop, and pressed me very much to prevail on my comrades to accept them. His design, as we afterwards learned, was, to make prisoners of us, hoping that disorder would take place among the soldiers next day when they should find themselves without their officers.

I immediately refused the offer. The priest asked me if I harboured any resentment for what had passed in the morning, and if we mistrusted the intentions of the inhabitants? I answered that we felt neither resentment nor distrust. He then begged me to go alone to his house at least, saying he would treat me well: I went to consult my comrades, and we agreed that I should go to the village alone to shew the inhabitants that we had no scheme of revenge, and thus to prevent them from thinking of attacking us in the night. My comrades were in hopes that I should be able to send them some supper. I returned to the priest; I asked him to give me his sacred word that no harm should be done to me; he gave it readily, and to prove how entirely I trusted him, I left my sword with the sentry and followed him unarmed.

We crossed the middle of the little town together; all the inhabitants whom we passed saluted my guide respectfully, and then looked at me with a threatening air. When they came too near so as to make me fear a surprise, the priest instantly repulsed them with a single look and frown, such was the authority which the sacred character with which he was invested gave him.

We soon arrived at his house, and were received by the minister's housekeeper: she was a tall woman of thirty-five or forty years of age. She first presented us with chocolate and biscuits, and then served up our meal on a table near the kitchen chimney. I sent some supper to my comrades, and sat down to table; the priest placed himself opposite, and the housekeeper sat at his right hand almost under the chimney-piece which was very high. After a moment's silence, the priest asked me if I was not going to mass the next day before I set out; I answered that I was not a Roman Catholic.

At these words his features contracted; and the house-keeper, who had never seen a heretic, shuddered on her chair, made an involuntary exclamation, heaved a profound sigh, and after having rapidly muttered several Ave Marias between her teeth, she consulted the priest's countenance, as a guide to the impression she should receive from so terrible an apparition as that of a heretic. (The popular descriptions and the church pictures of the country represent heretics breathing flames from their mouths.) The house-keeper recovered from her agitation when she saw the minister quietly resume the conversation.

After supper the priest invited me to sleep at his house, telling me that I must be tired, and that he would give me a bed at least as good as the bivouac. Seeing that I hesitated in my answer, he added, that it would be as well to let the crowd disperse, and that I must wait some hours. I then began to fear that he intended to keep me in his house in order to give me up to the inhabitants. I was afterwards told that such had really been his intention, and that he was the leader of the insurrection. Long after some reasons induced me to believe that by detaining me as his own prisoner, he wished to save me from the fate destined by the inhabitants of the village for our whole detachment.

As he had it in his power to betray me if he pleased, I took care not to shew him any distrust. I told him that I accepted his offers, believing myself in perfect safety since I was under the safeguard of his sacred word and that I would sleep, but I begged him to call me in two hours at farthest, because if my comrades did not see me return before midnight, they might come from their quarters and set fire to the whole village. The priest shewed me into the next room. I went to bed, a thing which rarely happened to us in Spain, and he carried away the lamp as he bade me good night.

The excessive darkness did not contribute to make me look upon the best side of the situation in which I found myself. I reproached myself for having quitted my sabre, and regretted it as a faithful companion which might have inspired me with good counsel. I heard the murmurs of the inhabitants in the street passing and repassing the windows. The priest opened my door from time to time, put in his grey head and the lamp in his right hand to see if I were asleep. I pretended to be soundly sleeping, and he went out gently.

Several men entered the next room; they at first talked calmly enough, and then confusedly all at once; then they became suddenly silent as if they were afraid of waking me, and of my listening to what they were saying; they then began again in an under voice, with great vehemence. I passed near two hours in this uncertain and whimsical situation, reflecting on the part I was to act. I at length determined to call the priest, and he immediately came. I told him that I wished to join my detachment immediately. He left his lamp without answering and quitted me, doubtless in order to consult the Spaniards who were in his house upon what was to be done with me.

Just at this time I experienced the most lively pleasure on seeing our quartermaster, who spoke Spanish, enter my room, accompanied by the *corregidor*. He told me that my companions were in the greatest anxiety about me, and that they had sent him to learn what had become of me; that the townspeople looked upon me as their prisoner; that they were to attack us the next day, and said that not one should escape. I dressed myself hastily, and called upon the priest again to keep his word, telling him that my comrades threatened to take up arms if I did not soon go back. Happily for me the preparations for the insurrection in the village were not completed; the priest dared not detain me any longer, and he called the *corregidor* and an *alcade* with a few men who placed us in the midst of them, and conducted us through the crowd to our bivouac.

The quartermaster whom my comrades had sent to me was a Norman, brave as his sabre. Under the appearance of the most perfect frankness, he concealed all the address commonly imputed to his countrymen. He had ingratiated himself with the inhabitants, by telling them that he was the son of a Walloon officer kept prisoner in France along with King Charles IV; that he had been forced to serve with us, and that he had long sought an opportunity of deserting. The Spaniards of the mountains were by turns cunning and credulous as savages. They believed the quartermaster, pitied him, gave him money, and revealed to him a part of their projects. By his means it was that we learned that the inhabitants of the neighbouring villages were to unite the next day in considerable numbers to attack us in a dangerous pass on the road to Ronda. This happy discovery saved us from total destruction.

The priest and the *corregidor* came to us, just as we were setting off the next day, to ask for an attestation to prove to any French troops who might come to Olbera that they had behaved well to us. They were in hopes that the threatening aspect of the townspeople would make us comply with their wishes. We answered that we could not give them such an attestation till they should have returned the arms taken from the horse belonging to the trooper who had shut himself up with me in the town-house the day before. We had already claimed them several times in vain.

The priest and the *corregidor* walked silently back towards the upper part of the village, and a few moments after their departure we heard cries of alarm. The townspeople had just murdered six hussars and two farriers who had imprudently gone to a smithy to shoe their horses; the musketry then was heard.

We mounted hastily, and the body of the detachment

followed the adjutant who commanded us, to the place of rendezvous about a musketshot from the village. I remained at the bivouac, and kept with me ten hussars to cover the retreat, and to protect the baggage which we had not yet got upon the backs of the mules, because the Spanish muleteers had fled in the night.

One of my comrades soon came back to tell me that our rearguard was on the point of being surrounded, and that the Spaniards kept up a brisk fire of musketry upon the detachment from the rocks and from the windows of the houses at that end of the village which we must pass. Having no hope of succour we resolved to cut our way through the enemy. My horse received a ball through his neck and fell. I succeeded in raising him immediately and reached the detachment. Shortly afterwards my comrade had his arm broken; we saw almost all the hussars fall successively round us. Women, or rather furies let loose, threw themselves with horrible shrieks upon the wounded, and disputed who should kill them by the most cruel tortures. They stabbed their eyes with knives and scissors, and seemed to exult with ferocious joy at the sight of their blood. The excess of their just rage against the invaders of their country seemed to have entirely changed their nature.

Meantime the detachment had remained motionless facing the enemy to wait for us. The natives dared not quit the rocks and houses, and we could not go with our horses to them to revenge the death of our companions. We called over our people before them; we placed the wounded in the centre of the troop and began our march slowly.

Not having been able to procure a guide, we took the first path which led off the beaten road where we knew the mountaineers had placed ambuscades, and we wandered for some time in the fields without knowing where we were. We then saw a man on a mule riding from a farm; I rode after him, reached him, and placing him between two of the advanced guard, ordered him, under pain of being put to the sword, to guide us to Ronda. Without this peasant, whom we met by chance, we should never have found our way in these unknown countries. It is thus that we had to struggle for ever against difficulties, not military and foreseen, such as are met with in regular war, but against numberless obstacles which, springing from the national character alone, were renewed and infinitely multiplied according to circumstances at every step.

We had hardly entered a pretty long valley, when we perceived on the heights towards our left a troop of a thousand or fifteen hundred persons watching our march. We distinguished among the number women and even children. They were the inhabitants of Setenil and the neighbouring villages, who, learning that we had changed our route in order to avoid their ambuscades, had set off in pursuit of us. They were running very fast in hopes of cutting off our march at a pass in front of us.

We pushed on our horses that they might not succeed, and fortunately passed the defile. We were soon after surrounded by a cloud of peasants detached from the main body, in great disorder and whose fire just reached our flanks. They followed us along the rocks without daring to approach nearer than musket-shot for fear of not being able to regain the mountain if we charged. Priest and *alcades* were riding on horseback along the heights to direct the movements of the crowd. Such of our wounded as had the misfortune to fall off their horses were stabbed behind us without mercy. One alone escaped, for he had the presence of mind to give the bystanders to understand that he wished to confess before he died, and the priest of Setenil saved him from the fury of his enemies.

When we had reached a narrow path, practised in the side of a steep mountain, we stopped a few minutes to breathe our horses; some rocks sheltered us from the fire of the enemy above us. At length we perceived Ronda, and just as we were rejoicing at being at length near the end of our journey, we were very much astonished to see new enemies firing from an ambush in the woods near the town. We then felt the greatest uneasiness lest it should have been abandoned by the French, but we soon saw, with the most lively joy, a party of hussars from our own regiment coming to meet us. They had mistaken us at a distance for enemies.

We entered the town and stopped in the great square. There our comrades came to embrace us, and to ask for news of France and the rest of the world from which they had been so long separated. We then dispersed into the different lodgings assigned for us, depending upon at least a few days' rest after the long fatigues we had just undergone.

The city of Ronda is situated in the midst of the high mountains one must cross in order to reach Gibraltar, and which are generally comprehended under the name of Sierra de Ronda. Their tops are entirely stripped of vegetation, and their sides covered with a sort of scaly rock which one might fancy had been for ages blackened and calcined by the heat of the sun. It is only at the bottom of the valleys and on the banks of the rivers that orchards and meadows are to be seen. Near the sea the vine spreads itself along the ground almost without culture, and from thence come the best Spanish wines.

Accustomed to struggle continually with the difficulties of savage nature, the inhabitants of these barren mountains are sober, persevering, and unconquerable; religion is their only bond of social union, and almost the only motive which restrains them. The ancient government of Spain was never able to subject them to the strict observance of the laws during peace, nor to make them serve in the armies during war, for they desert whenever they are led far from home.

The inhabitants of each village elect their own *alcades* for two years; but these magistrates seldom dare use their authority lest they should make enemies, and expose themselves to vengeance, which is there always implacable. If the king's judge were to pretend to use force to put an end to a quarrel, he would instantly see the poniard turned against himself; but if a spectator begins a prayer, it rarely happens that the combatants refuse to set aside their fury, and to join in it together, and in the most violent disputes the arrival of the holy sacrament always re-establishes good order.

I have been told that no great feast is ever given in the Sierra without two or three persons being stabbed. Among the men jealousy is a rage that nothing but the sight of blood can appease; the mortal blow almost always follows the sidelong look of anger.

These mountaineers are almost universally smugglers. They sometimes unite in pretty large troops from different villages, under the most famous of their chiefs, and they go down into the plains where they disperse to sell their goods, when they often resist troops sent in pursuit of them. These smugglers have always been famous for their address, and for the dexterity with which they elude the watchfulness of the numerous excise officers under the crown. Night and day roaming among their mountains, they know the most hidden caverns, the most rocky defiles, and the narrowest passes.

While the men are constantly occupied with this kind of smuggling war, their wives remain at home among the mountains, and do not shrink from undertaking the most laborious employments. They carry heavy burdens with ease, and boast of the superior strength given them by habit. They have been seen wrestling together and striving who should lift the heaviest stones. When they come down to Ronda, they are easily distinguished by their gigantic size, their robust limbs, and their looks which are at once full of wonder and boldness. When they come to the town they are fond of dressing in the finest stuffs and veils, which they obtain by smuggling, and which form a curious contrast with their dark sunburnt complexions and the coarseness of their features.

The warlike natives of these high mountains had all taken up arms against the French, and when King Joseph with his guards came to Ronda about three weeks before us, he had in vain tried first by persuasion and then by force to make them submit to his authority.

King Joseph remained but a few days at Ronda; he left 250 of our regiment, and 300 of his own foot-guards to garrison the place; and on leaving it, he gave unlimited power over the neighbouring provinces, with the title of civil and military governor, to our colonel. The absolute authority attached to this pompous title, equivalent with that of captain-general, was meant to extend over all the country fifteen or twenty leagues round, but the smugglers of the Sierra shut up our power within the narrow limits of the walls of Ronda, where we could not even sleep in peace, for we could not trust the inhabitants of the suburbs.

On the night after we arrived we saw a multitude of fires lighted successively on the neighbouring mountains. The illusion produced by the darkness brought even the most distant of the fires near us, and we might say that we were surrounded by a circle of flames. The enemy had just posted themselves round the whole town in order to attack us the next day.

For about half an hour we heard the sound of a goat's horn several times repeated, and which seemed to come from an olive grove below us, in a little valley without the old town. We were making a thousand jests of these unformed sounds, without being able to guess their meaning, when a hussar from one of our advanced posts galloped up to tell the colonel that a deputy from the enemy demanded entrance. The colonel gave orders to introduce him, and the trooper soon brought him with a bandage over his eyes. The deputy told us that he came to invite us to surrender; that the general of the mountain troops with 15,000 men occupied every outlet by which we might hope to escape; that a few days before he had taken a convoy of 50,000 cartridges which were designed for us, and that he knew we could not long keep the place because we had very little ammunition left. This was true; the infantry in the garrison had only three rounds a man, the hussars could make no use of their sabres among rocks, and their horses were more frequently an embarrassment than an assistance.

The colonel answered the deputy that we would first sit down to table, and made a sign to me to take our new guest into the room where our meal was prepared, telling me to take care of him. The deputy was a young man and rather good-looking; he wore the round Andalusian hat, and a short vest of brown cloth edged with a sky-blue chain lace; his only mark of distinction was a scarf in the fashion of the country, with a few silver threads at the end. Instead of a sabre he wore a long straight sword like the ancients.

He was for a moment surprised to find himself in his modest dress among a set of officers covered with embroidery, and when we all put our hands to our swords at the same time to take them off in order to sit down to table, he showed some uneasiness, not being aware of the cause of so sudden a motion. I fancy that the thought occurred to him that we were going to kill him by way of reprisal, because the inhabitants of a neighbouring village had murdered an attorney belonging to Ronda whom we had sent out as a deputy a few days before. I soon restored his confidence by inviting him to disarm himself and sit down with us.

After a few moments' silence I asked him if he had long been in the service of Ferdinand VII; he told me only a year, and that he entered as lieutenant in the Cantabrian hussars.

'Although we are enemies,' said I, 'we are doubly comrades, by rank and by using the same weapon.' He was much flattered by being considered as an officer in a regular troop.

I then asked some questions concerning the leaders of the insurgent army; he spoke much of the merits of General Gonzales, and said that he was a man of rare talents in the art of war, and that he possessed the most profound knowledge of tactics. We had never heard of him, but we afterwards learned that he was a serjeant of the line to whom the insurgents had lately given the rank of brigadier-general to make us believe that they had a regularly organized army.

At length, by praising extravagantly everything belonging in his party he told us the only thing it was of any importance for us to learn, by saying nothing about it which was, that no English troops from Gibraltar had joined the mountaineers: had they alone done so our situation would have been truly perilous.

The Spanish officer did not at first forget the characteristic sobriety of the nation, but when we drank his health he pledged us, and then piqued himself on drinking equally with us: we were only comrades in the middle of supper, but we were brothers at the dessert: we vowed eternal friendship, and among other marks of attachment we promised to fight in single combat the next time we met.

When supper was over the colonel sent the Spanish deputy back without an answer; I was commissioned to see him as far as the enemy's advanced post. I told him to tie the bandage over his eyes himself; a hussar on his right hand led his horse, I was on his left, and we went along the Gibraltar road by which he had come in. At our main-guard we were joined by the deputy's trumpeter, and by an old royal carabineer who was his orderly. This was the only carabineer they had in the insurgent army, and they had sent him as a mark of honour with the deputy on account of his new uniform. I was a good deal surprised at hearing him ask his officer in an authoritative tone why he had kept him so long waiting.

The deputy's trumpeter was a young shepherd whom they had dressed in a green cassock, which formed a singular contrast with his sandals, his bonnet, and the rest of his rustic habiliments; they had given him a lesson before they sent him to us. When the hussars asked him what he had done with his trumpet, he answered that he had lost it. He had, in reality, thrown away the modest shepherd's horn which he had blown, for fear the sight of so unmilitary an instrument should destroy the illusion that he was in hopes his disguise would produce.

The shepherd could not make his horse go on, for it kicked and stopped at every step. I called to him in Spanish to go on; but he answered sorrowfully, 'This is the first time I ever was on horseback, and they have given me a cursed brute which will not stir.' The carabineer, who was a few paces behind, came up, told the shepherd roughly to hold his tongue, and put an end to his perplexity by taking his horse's bridle.

When we reached the first Spanish post at the end of the suburb of the old town I bid the deputy adieu, and returned to give an account of my mission to the colonel. We held a council of war, and it was agreed that we should quit the place and go to wait for ammunition at Campillos, a small town situated seven leagues from Ronda at the skirts of the mountains, in a plain where our cavalry would give us a certain advantage over the mountaineers, however numerous. We had but little confidence in King Joseph's 300 guards, for they were for the most part Spanish deserters.

The colonel ordered the garrison to be ready to march within an hour without beat of drum or sound of trumpet, that the enemy might have no notice of our departure. I

141

immediately gave orders to the quartermasters who were under my command, and we went from house to house to awaken the conscripts of the detachment which had arrived with me. They had trusted to staying some time at Ronda to rest after the fatigues of their journey, and when we went at midnight to awaken them they were dead asleep, and not hearing the trumpet as usual they would not believe what we said. Some of them took us for the ghosts of their lieutenant and corporals coming to torment them even in their dreams with orders to march. We were obliged to strike them pretty smartly to prove that we were 'true men'.

For two hours we marched in the deepest silence, by the light of the olive wood fires which the mountaineers had kindled on the declivities of the neighbouring hills. At daybreak we stopped for a quarter of an hour on a small plain where we could have made use of our sabres, in order to see if the enemy had followed us; but they everywhere went away as soon as we approached, and regained the tops of the hills without choosing to come to action. The peasants from the villages near the road fired at us from time to time and at all distances. The women placed themselves upon the rocks to see us pass below them, and to rejoice in our retreat. They sung patriotic songs, in which they wished destruction to all the French, the Grand Duke of Berg, and to Napoleon. The burden of the song was always the crowing of a cock, which is considered as the emblem of France.

VII

A T length we arrived at Campillos, and we soon perceived by the manner in which the inhabitants received us that the news of our losses at Olbera and our retreat from Ronda had reached the place before us. When I entered my lodging I was very ill received by my host. My servant having asked for a room for me, he showed him a damp black kind of hole looking into a back court. We had not been able to distribute rations on our first arrival, and the *alcade* had published an order enjoining the inhabitants to feed the soldiers who should lodge with them. My orderly asked the master of the house by signs to give him something to eat. I saw him bring, with an air of mockery, a very small table, on which there was a little bread and a few cloves of garlic. I heard him tell his wife that it was, 'Good enough for those dogs of Frenchmen, there is no need to keep terms with them now; they have been beaten, they are running away, and please God and the holy mother, not a man of them should be alive in two days.'

I made believe not to understand his curses, that he might not learn that I knew Spanish. I went out, and came back in an hour afterwards to my lodging, where I found five men belonging to the village sitting round and smoking segars. I discovered that they were in the habit of meeting every evening at the house of my host who sold tobacco.

My hussar was at some distance from them; he arose on my entrance and offered me his chair. I accepted it, and drew it near the fire. The Spaniards at first became silent, but one of them asked me if I was tired, in order to discover whether I understood Spanish; and although I appeared not to comprehend him, he added with a sneer, 'You have made good use of your spurs these two days past.' I did not answer, so they thought that I did not know a word of Spanish, and resumed their conversation.

They spoke with boundless enthusiasm of the brave mountaineers who had driven us from Ronda. They related the minutest details of a supposed battle which had taken place the day before in the streets of that town. They told each other that we had lost at least six hundred men, while we had but five hundred and fifty in all. They affirmed that the mountaineers and their general were coming to attack us in two days at farthest; that the inhabitants of the village would take up arms, and that they would annihilate these damned heretics who were worse than the Moors; for the French, as they said, neither believed in God nor the Virgin, nor Saint Anthony, nor even in Saint James of Galicia, and made no scruple of lodging in churches with their horses. They repeated a thousand other invectives of the same kind, with which they raised their imaginations, and concluded by saying that a single Spaniard was worth three Frenchmen, and one of them said he would kill half a dozen with his own hand.

I then rose and said to them twice over, *poco a poco*; they were petrified at finding that I had understood their whole conversation. I left them to go and give the colonel notice of what I had heard; he immediately ordered the *alcade* to disarm the village. The inhabitants gave up their useless arms, and kept such as were serviceable, as it always happens in similar cases.

On returning to my lodging I did not find one of my politicians; they had all fled. My host had also hidden himself. His wife in consternation had endeavoured to conciliate my hussar during my absence: at first she had only given him water to drink, but she then brought him some excellent wine. He, who had no idea that fear had produced these attentions, was not a little surprised at this unhoped-for favour; his vanity began to rise, and I found him stroking up his horrible whiskers with more than ordinary complacency.

The moment I put down my sabre my host's wife took it up and carried it officiously to the finest room in the house, to take possession as it were in my name. She then came and tremblingly entreated me not to harbour resentment against her husband, telling me that although he had not received me well at first, that he was a respectable man, and that he had a very good heart.

I assured her that her husband might come back, that I would do him no harm on condition that he would give me timely notice of whatever he should learn concerning the projects either of the enemy or the inhabitants. I added, however, that if he failed I would certainly have him hanged, and I went to bed.

I rose next day at daybreak, and when I opened the door of my room, I perceived my host, who was waiting to make his peace with me. Before he said any thing, he presented me with a cup of chocolate and biscuits. I accepted it with a very condescending air, and told him, that I should be guided for the future in my conduct towards him by his behaviour to me. He answered, with a low bow, that he and his house were at my disposal.

On that day, the 15th March, we learned that the Serranos had entered Ronda an hour after we left it, and that they were preparing to attack us at Campillos.

145

On the 16th our colonel sent a detachment of a hundred hussars and forty foot soldiers, to reconnoitre the enemy. I went on the expedition, and we began our march two hours before sunrise, and met the mountaineers four leagues from Campillos. They had passed the night at a bivouac on the declivity of a hill near the village of Canete la Real. We stopped two musket shots from them to examine their position and to ascertain their number, which we reckoned to be about four thousand; and when we had finished our examination, we quietly turned back by the road by which we came.

The Serranos, seeing us turning round, fancied we were frightened at them; and began shouting aloud, running down the hill all together, and without observing any order, followed us for an hour in a difficult, and very much cut up country; the ground then became favourable for cavalry, their ardour subsided, and they stopped on the heights to re-assemble, not daring to advance into the plain.

They then sent some peasants to fire upon the skirmishers of our rearguard, who had faced about while the infantry and the body of the detachment crossed a wooden bridge thrown over a torrent which runs at the foot of a barren mountain, on the summit of which the village of Teba is perched like an eagle's nest.

The women of the village, dressed, according to the custom of the country, in pale blue and red clothes, had seated themselves on their heels, on the tops of the rocks, in order to see from a near and safe place the battle which they expected to take place. Our rearguard soon assembled its riflemen and began to cross the bridge: the women then rose all at once, and sung the hymn to the Virgin Mary. At this signal the fire began, and the Spaniards, hidden by the shoulder of the hill, poured upon us a shower of balls of every description; we continued to cross the bridge quietly under the fire of the enemy without returning it, we saw the women come down the rocks, tear the guns from their husbands' hands, and placed themselves before them to force them to advance and to pursue us beyond the bridge.

Our rearguard, feeling itself too close-pressed, faced about, and the hussars of the first line directed a fierce carbine fire against the nearest of the mountaineers, and killed two, which checked the impetuosity of the crowd, and the women precipitately returned to the top of the hill; but a hundred of the insurgents followed us at a little distance to within half a league of Campillos.

The next day, the 17th, a detachment of fifty hussars sent to reconnoitre, found the Serranos encamped on the other side of the wooden bridge below the village of Teba. The hussars advanced very near the bridge, and returned without firing a single shot. The enemy grew bold as they had done the day before, and followed our scouts as far as the advanced posts. Our intention was to draw them on to the plain near Campillos, and cut them to pieces. The insurgents being for the most part armed only with fowling-pieces, had always the advantage in the mountains, where we could not pursue them through the rocks; but in the plain their disorderly way of fighting did not allow them to sustain the shock of a charge of cavalry, however inferior in number.

At ten o'clock in the morning I saw my host arrive in great haste. A smile was on his lips, but he was rubbing his eyes endeavouring in vain to weep. He told me that all was lost for us, that our guards were repulsed, that fifteen hundred mountaineers were coming furiously down to the plain in order to surround us, while the revolted inhabitants should attack us in the centre of the village; and he pressed me closely in his arms as if he pitied the fate which threatened me.

The report of muskets, confused cries, and the sound of

trumpets and drums were in fact heard at the same instant. The people were running from all quarters to arms; one of our posts placed not far from the house I lived in had just been forced to retire to the entrance of the village. I immediately mounted my horse and collected my detachment. The colonel appeared at the same moment, and ordered me to go and support the repulsed guards. We made a charge in various directions in the plain, which succeeded; forty of our hussars cut a hundred of the mountaineers to pieces and those who were on the neighbouring heights fled in the greatest consternation. We then returned, and the plain which had before echoed to the shouts of a cloud of riflemen, remained silent and strewed with the scattered enemy who had just been cut down.

While we were on horseback repelling the enemy, the inhabitants, persuaded that we were to be annihilated, had murdered all our soldiers who had neglected to repair to the place appointed for rendezvous in case of danger. On returning to the village the hussars cut down every native whom they found armed, and there was some difficulty in preventing plunder. From that time the mountaineers did not dare to shew themselves in the plain; they marched the rest of the day and part of the night, without stopping, and regained their high mountains in the neighbourhood of Ronda.

On the 19th March, General Peremont came from Malaga to join us at Campillos with three battalions of infantry, a regiment of lancers from the Vistula, and two pieces of cannon. We received the ammunition we were in need of, and on the 20th, at six o'clock in the morning, we set off all together to take possession of Ronda once more. We went a little out of our road to levy a contribution on the inhabitants of Teba to punish them for having taken up arms against us three days before, although they had sent in their submissions to King Joseph.

Our colonel left his regiment at the foot of the hill, on the top of which Teba stands, and went to the village with only fifty hussars. The inhabitants, who had heard of our approach and of the contribution we meant to claim, had fled into their rocky fastnesses with their most precious effects. Clothes scattered up and down marked the traces of their precipitate flight.

The colonel gave orders to break open the doors of some of the houses in the market-place to see if we might find any of the inhabitants concealed. Only one old man was found, who, far from being afraid, shouted for joy as he saw the hussars enter his house. They were willing to have taken advantage of his good will towards them, and led him out that he might give them information, but they soon discovered that he was mad, and it was probably this misfortune which prevented his relations or friends from carrying him with them to the mountains.

We passed near two hours in the village without finding a single individual whom we could depute to the inhabitants to quiet them and assure them that no harm should be done to any one of them, but that they should be pardoned on condition that they would pay a contribution in the name of King Joseph. We did not wish to make irreconcileable enemies of them or to drive them to despair by rigorous punishment, yet it was of consequence not to leave their revolt wholly unchastised.

The following expedient was employed to draw them from their retreats. The hussars burned some wet straw in the chimneys of some of the houses; these fires produced a thick smoke, which, driven by the wind towards the mountain, persuaded the inhabitants that we were going to set fire to the village. They immediately sent a deputation, and we soon saw the *alcade*, followed by four of the richest natives, arrive. He wore a red cloak and a laced coat. He had doubtless put on all the marks of his dignity, because he expected to sacrifice his life for the safety of the village when he came to the French. The *alcade* promised that the inhabitants would pay the contribution we demanded. We carried him with us as a hostage, and he returned home two days afterwards.

The same night we slept at a little village only four leagues from Campillos. On the 21st we set out at sunset for Ronda, which we entered without resistance. The mountaineers abandoned the town precipitately at our approach, and threw down their guns and cloaks in the streets that they might the more readily gain the mountain through by-paths. The hussars of our advanced guard cut down the last of the fugitives.

We were received as deliverers by a part of the inhabitants of Ronda. During our absence the mountaineers had erected a gallows in the principal square in order to punish such of the townspeople as had favoured the French; and if we had come a day later several individuals would have been led to execution, and thus private animosities would have been satisfied under pretence of public justice. A magistrate was to have been hanged because he would not receive a bribe in a case of smuggling, years before; and a poor tailor was thrown upon the rocks and dashed to pieces the night preceding our return, because he had served as interpreter to our soldiers.

The very day on which we left Ronda, the mountaineers entered it by daybreak, shouting with joy and discharging their pieces exultingly in the streets. The inhabitants of each village arrived together marching without order, and followed by their wives, only distinguishable from the men by their dress, their greater stature, and their coarser manners.

They pretended that their husbands had taken Ronda by conquest from the French, and that everything in the town belonged to them: they said to each other, stopping proudly before the doors of the best houses, 'I take this house; I shall be a lady, and come to take possession in a few days with my goats and my children.' In the meantime they loaded their asses with whatever they found in the apartments; and these *ladies* did not cease plundering till the poor beasts were ready to sink under the weight of the booty.

Some smugglers stole an English lieutenant's horses and portmanteau, though he was with them on their expedition, but he could by no means bring the guilty persons to punishment. The prisons were forced, and the insurgents and criminals they contained ran instantly to take revenge on their judges and their accusers. Debtors obtained receipts from their creditors by forcible means, and all the public papers were burned, in order to annul the mortgages that the inhabitants of the town had upon the property of any of the mountaineers.

The commander-in-chief of the Serranos did not reach Ronda till six hours after our departure from it. By the assistance of what he called his regular troops, he endeavoured to establish some kind of order in the town, but not being able to succeed, he made use of the following stratagem: He caused the public crier to proclaim that the French were coming back. The mountaineers instantly assembled, and the inhabitants had time to barricade their houses.

The person who possessed the greatest influence over these undisciplined hordes was a man of the name of Cura, a native of Valencia, where he had been professor of mathematics. Having killed a man in a fit of jealous phrenzy, he was forced to become an exile from his country, and to take refuge among the mountain smugglers in order to escape the search of justice. He had contrived to have it whispered that he was a person of the most exalted birth, but that for reasons of state he was forced to keep himself unknown.

151

The mountaineers had surnamed him the 'stranger with the wide bonnet', because he affected to wear the cap of the country of an extraordinary size, in order to attract notice, which, along with this kind of mystery, gave him great power over men's minds. The 'stranger with the wide bonnet', however, having raised heavy contributions upon several mountain villages about a month afterwards, under pretence of buying arms and ammunition, attempted to make his escape with the money which had been entrusted to him, but he was taken and punished.

General Peremont had led his brigade to Ronda for the purpose of making an expedition from thence into the heart of the mountains, but he was forced to return to Malaga, without having attempted any thing. He learned that the last mentioned city had been attacked during his absence by other insurgent troops, and therefore left our regiment of hussars to garrison Ronda a second time, and instead of the battalion of King Joseph's guards which served with us before, he gave us two hundred of the bravest Polish infantry.

The town of Ronda is situated on a crag which is very easy of access and only steep on the north side. It is separated from the mountains which command it towards the south and west, by a fertile and well cultivated valley. The Guadiaro descends from the highest of these mountains, and runs through Ronda; one would imagine that a violent earthquake had cleft the high crag on which the town is built, in order to form the deep dark bed of this little river.

The old town, situated on the left bank of the river, communicates with the new town on the opposite bank by a superb stone bridge of a single arch. Iron balconies project beyond the parapet on each side; and one is struck with a kind of terror when suddenly through the thin iron bars one discovers the river, two hundred and seventy-six feet below one, like a single white thread running out of the gulf which the violence of the torrent must have formed ages back. A sort of misty damp is always rising from the abyss, and the eye can hardly perceive at that immense distance the men and asses who are continually climbing up and down the winding pathway to carry burdens to the different mills constructed at the foot of the immense rocky terrace which supports the town.

From the tops of these rocks we often saw, during these times of war and trouble, the gardeners of the valley quitting their peaceful labours to join the mountaineers when they came to attack us; or perceived them bury their guns on the approach of a Frenchman.

That part of Ronda which is called the old town is almost entirely of Moorish construction, the streets being narrow and winding; but the new town is, on the contrary, regularly built; the squares are large and the streets wide and straight. We easily put the old town in such a state of defence as to guard it against a surprise, by constructing a few works and repairing an old castle which our foot soldiers were fully equal to defending, and our hussars were specially entrusted with the care of the new town. We threw down some old walls, and levelled some inequalities in the approach to that side in order to be able to repulse the enemy by a charge of cavalry in case of need.

The mountaineers had encamped on the neighbouring heights, and watched day and night what was doing in the town. When our trumpets sounded the reveillée at sunrise, the shepherd's horn was soon heard rousing the mountaineers on the tops of the neighbouring hills. They passed whole days in annoying our outposts in different ways, but the moment we made a sally they retired, only to return and harass us anew.

Whenever the Serranos prepared for an attack, they shouted aloud to animate each other for the fight, and fired on us long before their balls could reach us. Such as were farthest off fancied, on hearing the firing and the shouts, that their companions in front had gained an advantage. They accordingly pressed forward to join in the action and partake the honour of the success which they believed to be easy; they often in their eagerness got before those who at first had held the foremost ranks, and when they discovered their error, it was too late to go back. We allowed them to come as far as the little plain round the new town, as it gave us an opportunity of charging and cutting them down, but they always retreated as soon as they had lost a few of their men.

The most popular pastime among the labourers of Ronda was to sit on the rocks among the olive groves at the end of the suburb and smoke segars while they fired upon our videttes. In the morning they would go out of the town with their tools, as if they were going to work in the fields, but there or at the farmhouses they found their guns, and returning them at night they would come back to the town and sleep in the midst of us. It not unfrequently happened that our hussars recognised their hosts among their enemies, but it was impossible to make very rigorous searches, for if Marshal Soult's decree against insurgent Spaniards had been carried into execution, we must have punished nearly the whole population of the country with death. The mountaineers hung their French prisoners or burned them alive; and in return, our soldiers rarely gave quarter to a Spaniard found under arms.

The women, the old men, and even the children, were against us, and served as spies for the enemy. I saw a young boy of eight years old playing about among our horses' feet; he offered himself as a guide, and led a small party of hussars straight to an ambuscade. When he reached it he suddenly ran off towards the rocks, throwing up his bonnet in the air, and crying with all his might, 'Long live our

154

King, Ferdinand VII!' and the firing instantly began.

All that was wanting on the score of military discipline among the mountaineers, was amply made up by the strength and perseverance of their inflexible character. If they were no match for us in the plain, if they failed in attacks requiring great combinations, they in revenge fought admirably among rocks and behind the walls of their homes – in short, wherever we could not bring cavalry against them. We were never able to subdue the inhabitants of Montejaque, a little hamlet half a league from Ronda, and containing only fifty or sixty houses.

The inhabitants of every mountain town or village, who believed themselves exposed to the visits of the French, sent their old men, their women and their children to inaccessible fastnesses, and hid their most valuable property in caverns. The men remained alone in the places to defend them or to make secret incursions into the plains to carry off the cattle of such Spaniards as refused to declare themselves against us.

The little town of Grazalema was the arsenal of the mountaineers. Marshal Soult sent a column of 3,000 men against that small place. The smugglers defended themselves from house to house, and only abandoned the place for want of ammunition; they then escaped into the mountains, after having destroyed a considerable number of our soldiers, and the moment the army left the town they took possession again.

A division consisting of three regiments of the line, sent a month afterwards to disperse the insurgent army again, easily repulsed the mountaineers from every point in the open country, but they could not succeed in gaining possession of Grazalema. Some smugglers had entrenched themselves in the market-place, which is in the centre of the town; they had placed mattrasses before the windows of the houses in which they had shut themselves up. Twelve hussars of the 10th Regiment, and forty rifle-men who formed the advanced guard of the French division, arrived in the square without meeting with any resistance, but they never returned. Every one of them was struck by the fire which poured from the windows on all sides, and all who were sent to the same spot perished immediately in like manner, without having done the smallest damage to the enemy.

The expeditions which the French frequently sent against the highest part of the mountains almost always dispersed the enemy's troops without subduing them, and our parties returned to Ronda with great loss. Even when our troops were superior in number the Serranos baffled all their efforts by their manner of fighting in the mountains. On the approach of our compact bodies, they retreated from rock to rock and from position to position, without intermitting their fire or ceasing for a moment to harass us. As they fled they destroyed whole columns without giving us an opportunity of taking revenge. This manner of fighting had procured them the name of 'mountain flies', even from the Spaniards themselves, alluding to the manner in which those obstinate insects torment living beings without ever leaving them an instant's rest.

The detachments which went out of Ronda, either on necessary expeditions or to reconnoitre, were surrounded from the moment of their departure to that of their return to the town by a cloud of skirmishers. Every convoy of provisions which we brought from without cost us the lives of several men killed by ambuscades. We might with truth say in the language of Scripture, 'that we eat our own flesh and drank our own blood' in this inglorious war, in expiation of the injustice of the cause for which we were fighting.

The mountains of Grenada and Murcia were not more submissive than those of Ronda; and the French, attacked in every point of communication by the whole population, found themselves nearly in the same situation with our regiment in all the mountainous parts of the country. Such was the repose we enjoyed after having conquered Spain from the French frontiers even to the gates of Cadiz. The siege of that city was then the only military event worthy of attention.

When our horses had consumed the forage of all the farms in the neighbourhood of Ronda, we were obliged to extend our excursions, and to send parties of thirty or forty hussars to get cut straw several leagues from the town, three or four times a-week. The weakness of the garrison did not permit us to send detachments of infantry to support our foragers, as we too often felt it would have been expedient to do. Our horsemen were not always strong enough to repulse the enemy in these expeditions, and we sought to elude their vigilance either by taking a different road every day or by going a great way about to avoid the dangerous hill passes, and frequently we were obliged to cut our way through the insurgents, who were for ever collected round the town.

Fortune had been most favourable to me for a whole month. I succeeded in all enterprises without the town, and when it was my turn to do duty at the main-guard none of our people were ever killed. The hussars, who are in great measure fatalists, began to think me invulnerable. I was, nevertheless, almost mortally wounded on the 1st May; but I was since told, to comfort me, that fate had made a mistake; that I ought not to look upon myself as less fortunate than before, because the adjutant had made a mistake in arranging us on that service, and that I had marched in the place of one of my comrades who had an unlucky star.

On the 1st May I was with a detachment of forty-five hussars, commanded by a captain; we were going to seek cut straw a few leagues from Ronda, at some farms belonging to the village of Setenil and we were accompanied by about a hundred peasants and muleteers from the town to lead the mules and asses. We had set out at five o'clock in the morning, and the captain and I marched at the head of the troop. We said to each other, as we passed through a defile half a league from the town, the enemy must have been very ill advised not to have placed an ambuscade in that place before that hour, by which they might have done us a great of harm without running any risk themselves.

On going up a steep hill I saw at a distance what at first appeared to be a cloud of dust, but afterwards, distinctly on our right, four or five hundred armed men advancing in the valley towards the village of Ariate; I told the captain that I saw the enemy, and that I was sure of it by the haste and disorder of the march.

A quartermaster, however, asserted that the people we saw in the field were muleteers returning to Ossuna, and who had been the day before at Ronda to bring biscuit and cartridges, under an escort of two hundred men. I obstinately maintained that they were the enemy's troops, and added that if I commanded the detachment I would immediately charge them while they remained in the flat country, for if we were repulsed our retreat was secure, while we could not continue our march without exposing ourselves to being attacked on our return in some pass unfavourable to the cavalry. The captain was not of my opinion; we therefore went on, and soon arrived at the village of Setenil.

The slowness and ill-will of the Spanish muleteers who had accompanied us to load the mules, gave us some suspicions; and these suspicions increased when, just as we were preparing to return to Ronda, we saw a peasant on horseback on a hill at a little distance watch our marching, and then gallop off as if to give notice to the enemy. When we had done foraging, we set out again by the same road, sending on the mules before us between an advanced-guard of twelve hussars and the main body of the detachment, at the head of which I was with the captain. When we were about two musket-shots from the pass which we dreaded the most, I saw a peasant sitting in an olive tree cutting the branches very busily with a hatchet. I galloped on before the detachment, and approached the peasant to ask him if he had not seen the Serranos. I afterwards learned that he was one of them, and was cutting those branches to bar up the pass. He answered, affecting to go on eagerly with his work, that his employment did not leave him leisure to attend to what passed around him.

At the same moment the captain was questioning a child of five or six years old, whose answers were low and hesitating, as if he was afraid of being heard. But we had no time to pay attention to his confused tale, for we saw our advanced guard, at the head of the mules, come out of the other side of the pass, and go up the opposite hill: we had to go along a narrow and slippery path where we were obliged to march one by one, and which was five or six hundred paces long and bounded by very thick garden hedges.

The captain, by whose side I was marching, repeated what he had said in the morning, that it was lucky that the enemy had not placed any ambuscade in the pass. He had scarcely spoken the words when four or five shots from behind the hedge killed the three last mules of the convoy and the trumpeter's horse, which was before us; our horses instantly stopped.

The captain was to have marched on first, but the horse he rode had belonged to an officer who had been killed a few days before on a similar expedition, and the animal hesitated. Seeing this I spurred my horse and got before the captain; I leaped over the trumpeter's horse and the mules who had just fallen with their burthens, and passed the defile alone. The Serranos, who were placed behind the

159

hedges, thought the whole detachment was close behind me, and discharged all their pieces as I passed. Two balls only reached me, the first passed through my left thigh; the other entered my body.

The captain followed me at some distance and arrived safe and sound at the other side of the pass; and of the whole detachment there were only the four last men killed, because the enemy suspended their fire for a few minutes while they loaded their guns a second time. The quartermaster, who brought up the rear of the detachment, had his horse shot under him, and he counterfeited death himself, slipped into the brushwood, and came back in the middle of the night to Ronda without any wound.

When we had rallied, and formed our detachment in line, on the other side of the pass, I told the captain that I was wounded, that I felt my strength failing me, and that I was going to return to Ronda by a pretty steep cross road, which was very short. He advised me to remain with the detachment, which was going to take a road half a mile longer round the plain, where there was no enemy, that they might not expose themselves uselessly to a second attack. I felt that I could not support so long a march, and I entered the steep path preceded by a hussar, who led my horse by the bridle.

As I was losing blood, I was obliged to summon up all my strength that I might not faint; if I had fallen off my horse I should probably have been stabbed. I held by both hands to the pommel of my saddle, making vain efforts to push on my horse by spurring it with the only leg I had to use. The poor animal went no faster and staggered at every step, for a ball had passed through him.

When I was within a quarter of a league of the town my horse could scarcely move. The hussar who accompanied me galloped off to give notice to the outposts on the top of the hill, and I managed to get on a few paces alone, though scarcely able to see, or hear the peasants' guns, who were firing at me from a distance, while they were cutting wood. I was, at length, relieved by the arrival of some soldiers, who conveyed me to my lodgings in my horsecloth.

My Spanish hosts came to meet me, and would not allow me to be carried to the military hospital, where there was an epidemical fever; I should probably, like many others, have found death by way of cure. Till that day my hosts had behaved to me with cold and reserved politeness, looking upon me as one of the enemies of their country. Respecting their patriotism, I myself had been but little communicative with them. The moment I was wounded they showed me the most lively interest, and treated me with that charity and that generosity which so eminently distinguish the Spanish character. They told me, that since I could do no more harm to their country they considered me as one of their family; and without a single moment's intermission, they nursed and watched over me for fifty days.

At daybreak on the 4th May the insurgents came with a stronger force than they had ever yet assembled to attack Ronda. Balls passed so near my windows that they were obliged to move my bed into the next room. My host and hostess came to tell me, while they endeavoured to appear calm themselves, that the mountaineers were at the end of the street, that they were gaining ground towards us, and that the old town was on the point of being carried by storm: they added that they were going to take precautions to shelter me from the fury of the Serranos, till the arrival of General Lerrana Valdenebro, who was their relation, and they carefully hid my arms, my military dress, and whatever else might have attracted the attention of the enemy, and with the assistance of their servants, they carried me to the top of the house behind a little chapel dedicated to the Virgin Mary, looking on that consecrated place as an inviolable asylum. My hosts then brought two priests, who placed themselves at the street door to defend it, and, in case of need, to protect me by their presence.

An old lady, the mother of my hostess, remained alone with me, and began praying; she turned the beads of her rosary faster or slower according as the cries of the combatants or the noise of the firearms announced the increase or diminution of the danger. Towards noon the firing seemed farther and farther off, and at length ceased entirely. The enemy was repulsed from every point, and my comrades came to relate the particulars of the battle the moment they got off their horses.

A few days afterwards the second hussars received orders to go to Santa Maria; it was replaced by the 43rd Regiment of the Line, and I was the only one of my own corps left at Ronda; I did not know any of the officers of the new garrison, and I received no visits from the French, excepting indeed that a subaltern, the adjutant of a foot regiment, who was impatient for my quarters, came now and then to inquire of my host whether I was dead or well enough to set off yet.

After the departure of my comrades, my hosts redoubled their kindness and attention. They passed several hours every day in my room; and when I began to get a little better they invited a few of their neighbours every evening to come and talk, or sometimes to perform a little concert by my bedside, to make me forget my sufferings. They sung their national songs and accompanied themselves with the guitar.

The mother of my hostess had conceived a great friendship for me ever since the day she had remained in my room to pray fervently for my safety during the assault. Her second daughter was a nun in a convent of noble ladies; she sent to ask after my health from time to time, and sent me little baskets of perfumed lint, covered with rose-leaves.

The nuns of the different convents of Ronda had doubled

their prayers and penances from the time we entered Andalusia. They passed the greater part of their nights in praying for the success of the Spanish cause, and during the day they employed themselves in preparing medicines and comforts for the wounded French; this mixture of patriotism and Christian charity was not rare in Spain.

On the 18th June, I rose for the first time since my wound. I was obliged to begin my melancholy apprenticeship of walking with crutches; I had totally lost the use of one of my legs. I went to visit the horse who was wounded with me; he had got quite well, but he did not know me at first, which showed me how much I was changed.

On the 22nd I left Ronda on an ammunition cart, which was going to Ossuna to fetch cartridges, under a strong escort. I parted from my hosts with the same kind of regret that one feels on leaving the home of one's fathers for the first time. They also were sorry at my leaving them; they had become attached to me by the kindnesses with which they themselves had loaded me.

I went from Ossuna to Essica, and from Essica to Cordova. Bodies of Spanish partisans, three or four hundred strong, scoured the country on all sides: when pursued, they retreated either to the mountains which separate Andalusia from Estremadura and La Mancha; or to those of the sea coast. These troops of partisans or guerrillas served to keep alive the fermentation of the country, and kept up the communications between Cadiz and the interior of Spain. The people were led to believe that the Marquis de la Romana had beaten the French at Truxillo, and that the English in a sortie from Gibraltar had completely defeated them near the sea. These reports, however improbable, being skilfully spread, were received with transport; hope thus continually renewed, excited partial insurrections in various parts, and the news of imaginary success, spread at a fortunate moment, often procured real advantages.

At some distance from Cordova there was a long established band of robbers; thieves by profession, they ceased not to strip Spanish travellers, but that they might acquit themselves of the obligation that every citizen contracts at his birth to shed his blood for his country when invaded, they made war on the French and attacked their detachments even though certain of obtaining no booty.

On leaving Andalusia I crossed La Mancha; I was obliged to stop several days at every station to await the return of the escorts who convoyed ammunition regularly to the siege of Cadiz. Sometimes wearied with staying so long in bad quarters, I abandoned myself to fate and took the chance of going alone from one halting place to another. The commandants at the posts of communication could only give escorts for the indispensable service of the army, for they often lost several men in attempting to escort a single courier for a few leagues.

King Joseph had no regular means of levying his taxes; it was in vain that he sent his moveable columns to scour the country; the inhabitants fled to the mountains or defended themselves in their dwellings. The soldiers sacked the villages, but the contributions were not raised; peaceable individuals sometimes paid for all the rest, but they were afterwards grievously punished by the guerrilla chiefs, for not having fled also at the approach of the French. The inhabitants of La Mancha as well as those of the neighbouring provinces were exasperated by such violent measures, and the number of our enemies daily increased. New Castile, which I likewise passed through in my journey, was not more tranquil than La Mancha. Some Spanish partisans had been on the point of taking King Joseph prisoner in one of his country houses near Madrid.

I arrived at last in that capital, and there stayed, waiting a favourable opportunity of returning to France.

King Joseph gave bullfights several times a week to please

the people, attach them to his new government, and divert their attention from the presence of our armies. With this artful design he spared neither pains nor expense, and procured from Andalusia the most expert and renowned practitioners. The inhabitants of Madrid and the neighbourhood thronged to the spectacle, notwithstanding their habitual sadness and the calamities of the times.

Most travellers, who have written upon Spain, disdaining to enter into the customs of the Spaniards, or rather to divest themselves of their national prejudices, have represented the bullfights as only fit to excite horror and disgust in the mind of every civilised man. We might reduce to the same level certain pastimes of the ancients, and even those which still exist among some modern nations, were we to strip them of the recollections, the feelings, and habits which have consecrated them.

Tragedy, without the buskin which raises in our mind the actions represented, would be merely the tiresome and repulsive exhibition of treachery and murder. The chase, which is considered in our countries as the noblest of exercises, the greatest pleasure of kings, the chase would be merely a slaughter; instead of which it is the school and living picture of war; it teaches a contempt of danger and death; it instructs us to brave fatigue and the inclemencies of the weather, to study the seasons, to note the various changes of the ground, to conquer difficulties, to avoid insurmountable obstacles, to baffle, by superior intelligence, the cunning and numberless stratagems which nature has bestowed upon animals.

The Romans, conquerors and oppressors of the world, a people whose foreign power depended on the strictness of their discipline and superiority in the art of fighting man to man, flocked to the circus to see the combats of wild beasts, and the combats of a hundred, nay of five hundred gladiators against five hundred. These spectacles were the exact representations of war, given as festivals to the people with the view of weakening, by habit, their natural horror at the sight of blood, to accustom them to the contempt of death; in a word, to awaken in the citizens of Rome that warlike ardour which the beauty of the climate and the richness of the soil might destroy.

The origin of bullfights among the Spaniards is derived from the Moors, shepherds of Africa, a nation skilled in training horses, in managing unruly flocks, and conquering the wild beasts of the desert. The Spaniards inherit from the Moors the practice of a wandering life, which they have preserved even to our times. Throughout Spain there are extensive tracks left untilled for the travelling flocks. The king and the grandees have vast studs appropriated to the raising of choice breeds of horses and bulls. The royal stud of Aranjuez, on the banks of the Tagus, is fifteen or twenty leagues in circumference. Gentlemen formerly fought on the bull-festivals; but they seldom now present themselves in the arena, either because the manners of the age are become milder by time, or rather, perhaps, because the frequent abode in the capital and the pleasures of courts have extinguished for the moment in the Spanish nobles their inclination for such sports.

We should form a very wrong idea of the bull that is to fight, if we judged of him by those which are seen in some countries of the north straying innocently through the meadows round the herdsmen which guard them. He is not the friend, the peaceable companion of the husbandman, the ox accustomed to bow his head gently to the yoke fastened to his horns, to obey without a murmur the goad that spurs him on; he is the king of the forest, where he has lived, almost wild, under a meridian sun; a fiery blood boils in his veins, and excites him to anger. The hills and vales lately echoed with his lengthened bellowings. He is a proud conqueror accustomed to fight for the young heifer, to see

166

everything give way, and even men fly at his approach, or at the first sound of his formidable fury.

I saw pass one of the unruly animals that were to fight in the evening. He had been brought, it was said, from Salamanca; his dark rusty coat gave him an air of great ferocity; six powerful men could with difficulty hold him, by ropes sufficiently long to prevent danger. A young heifer preceded to entice him into the *tauril*, a dark, narrow enclosure furnished with trapdoors, in which the bulls are separately put till the time fixed for the fight. In this place their angry passions are still farther inflamed by different torments: on the upper part of the breast is placed a riband which denotes by its colour their origin, breed, and birthplace.

The bullfights at Madrid are given in an amphitheatre open at the top; the spectators are seated in rows and separated from the arena, which is in the centre, by a strong wooden fence. Boxes are constructed in the upper part of the edifice; places in the shade pay double the price of those that are exposed to the heat of the sum. The spectacle opens with a sort of parade executed by the horse and foot combatants, all richly dressed according to the old Spanish costume. The *picadores* fight on horseback, armed with lances; their horses are saddled in the Moorish fashion; the lances are furnished with a sharp four-cornered head, made so as to wound the bull, without entering deep into his body. The *chulos* fight on foot, armed with darts; their arm of defence is a piece of red cloth which, attracting by its glare the bull's eyes, enables the skilful to avoid his attacks, and baffle his fury by favour of this illusory buckler.

Flourishes are heard; the barrier opens, and the bull appears. He has to avenge the many injuries received in his dark prison and the craft by which he was entrapped; with his hair on end and nostrils on fire, he stamps the ground, and threatens with his horns the spectators; the solemn silence that instantly succeeds the thrilling sound of the trumpets, far from intimidating him, seems to increase his ardour. He surveys the arena, and, in three bounds, darts on the first picador that comes forward. The *picador*, firm in his seat, lowers his lance which he holds in rest, and, pulling round his horse, drives it into the bull's broad breast, just as their fierce adversary inclines his head, to make a dreadful blow. The shock is sometimes so violent that the lance shivers to pieces; and the bull suddenly stopped in his course, is forced backward with pain from the wound. Should the *picador*'s horse be thrown, one of the foot combatants approaches, and draws the bull from his victim by a red cloak; proud of his success, and attracted by the scarlet, the noble animal turns his rage against this new enemy, more formidable to appearance, and proportions his effort to the expected resistance: the *chulo* leaps aside, and leaves the cheated bull to roar and wreak his fury on the cloak left between his horns.

Every time the bull conquers a new enemy, he lifts his proud head, and casts a scornful and haughty look around him; calmed, for a while, by victory, he seems to delight in the repeated plaudits of the multitude, and listens with pleasure to the shouts of 'Bravo, Bull! Bravo, Bull!' that come from all parts of the amphitheatre.

The Picadores are succeeded by the *chulos* or *banderilleros*, who advance on foot. The bull attacked takes a fresh spring; he thinks, in one course, to free himself from this weak, light and nimble troop which unceasingly harasses him; but they everywhere open at his approach; the *banderilleros* pass and repass; adroitly plant their darts in the bull's neck and breast, and, by their extreme agility, sport with his fury. I have seen one of these *chulos*, too closely pursued to escape by leaping the fence, boldly place his foot between the bull's horns and, tossed by the blow that was intended for him, fall unharmed some paces behind.

The troop of *banderilleros* retires at a signal agreed upon, and the *matador* appears, to finish the fight by the bull's death; he holds a sword in his right hand, and a flag in his left. After a low bow before the magistrates' box, he turns round, advances with a firm and orderly step towards the bull, whose motions he several times studies, by presenting and withdrawing his flag. The spectators are suspended betwixt fear and hope; all eyes are fixed on the point of the *matador*'s sword, who must pay with his life his irresolution or want of skill, should his blow fail or his hand falter. At length he lifts his sword, and plunges it between the shoulders into the very heart of the bull, who, eager to strike the *matador*, closes, staggers, falls, and measures the ground with his huge body. The four-footed hero, victor in many battles, raises, for the last time, his dying head, and in one lengthened roar, the blood gushing from his mouth and nostrils, he expires.

Flourishes announced the bull's entrance, flourishes are again heard at the death. Three mules harnessed abreast and richly caparisoned come from a door opposite that by which the combatants entered, gallop to the bull, and drag him away with cords fastened to his horns.

The bull which comes next respires sometimes with frantic horror the still reeking blood scattered about the arena; and seized with the fury of revenge, he attacks indiscriminately all his foes at once. Sometimes too a timid bull wanders cowardly about the course, and returns to the outlet whence he came; but that is irrevocably shut. The spectators consider him unworthy the honour of fighting with men; the dogs are loudly called for, and the bull, assaulted by a pack, is soon thrown. He is struck on the head with a sharp-pointed instrument made for the purpose, and dies amid barkings, shoutings and abuse.

This bloody tragedy, of which the devoted bull is the chief actor, presents the living picture of war as it was before the invention of gunpowder. It offers to the mind its tumult, uncertainty and agitations, and the spectator, as in a field of battle, feels that electric emotion which is excited by the shedding of blood.

Directly the spectacle begins, an almost convulsive joy seizes the spectators of every age and of both sexes. In an instant the gravest countenances expand and become cheerful. The men, seated on benches, lean forward and open their cloaks to be more appropriate to the action, as if they were to take part in it. They are seen to follow with their eyes and gestures every motion of the *picador* or bull, and even encourage the animal by words, thinking thus to influence, by their own eagerness, the fate of the combat.

I remained near a month at Madrid, waiting for an opportunity of going on. It was easy to get there from Bayonne, because there were strong detachments constantly coming to reinforce the army; but none but those who were maimed obtained leave to return to France. The Board of Health had received the strictest orders to grant no furlow to any officer or man as long as there were any hopes of a cure. I was almost those sent back to France on these conditions; but I was glad, at any price, to quit an unjust and inglorious war, where the sentiments of my heart continually disavowed the evil my arm was condemned to do.

I left Madrid with a numerous caravan of reduced officers, who were going back to France under an escort of only seventy-five foot soldiers. We formed a little company of officers, commanded by the first wounded among us, that we might die in arms if we were attacked, for we could not think of defence, many being so badly wounded as to be obliged to be tied on their horses in order to keep them from falling.

We had two madmen among us. The first was a hussar officer, who had lost his senses in consequence of bad wounds on the head; he marched on foot; his horse and arms having been taken from him lest he should make his escape and do any mischief. Notwithstanding his madness he remembered the dignity of his rank and the name of his regiment; sometimes he uncovered his head before us, showing us real wounds, while he related the imaginary battles in which he fancied he had received them. One day that our escort was attacked during our march, he eluded the vigilance of the men who had been ordered to keep him, and recovered his accustomed bravery in order to fall upon the enemy with a small switch, which he called the magic wand of his predecessor the King of Morocco.

The second of our madmen was a Flemish musician of the light infantry, in whose brain the warmth of the Spanish wines had fixed imperturbable gaiety. He had changed his clarinet for a fiddle, which he had been accustomed to play while a boy at village feasts, and he marched in the midst of our melancholy troop, dancing and playing incessantly.

On the long and silent road no single traveller ever met our sight. Every two or three days a convoy of ammunition, or an escort met and joined us, to lodge in the ruins of deserted dwellings, whose doors and windows had been carried off to furnish firewood for the French army. Instead of the crowd of children and idle spectators which usually in time of peace meets strangers at the entrance of a country village, we now saw only a small French outpost which, from behind its palisade, would cry 'Halt!' in order to reconnoitre us. Sometimes also in a deserted village, a sentry would suddenly appear placed in an old tower, like a solitary owl among ruins.

The nearer we approached to France, the more danger we were in of being carried off by the partisans; at every station where we halted we found detachments from different parts of the Peninsula, waiting to march with us. Battalions, and even whole regiments reduced to skeletons, that is, to two or three men only, were sadly bringing back their eagles and their banners, to recruit in France, or Italy, or Switzerland, or Germany, or Poland. Our convoy left Spain at the end of July, twenty days after Ciudad Rodrigo fell into the hands of the French.

VIII

A ND here I ought to terminate these memoirs since, as I quitted Spain at that period of the war, I no longer saw it with my own eyes; but since that time, during a year's residence in England, I procured materials which could not then be collected on the continent; and I have permitted myself to add the account of the campaign of Portugal, the *chef-d'œuvre* of a defence at once national and military, to my own journal.

After the campaign of Austria, and the peace concluded at Vienna in 1809, France found herself delivered from all her wars in the north, and the whole of Europe once more believed that Spain and Portugal must shortly sink under the immense forces which the Emperor Napoleon had at his disposal. That conqueror had declared that he was going to drive the English out of the Peninsula, and that within twelve months his triumphant eagles should be planted on the towers of Lisbon; and he sent strong reinforcements into Spain, in order to invade Portugal.

The French army destined for this invasion consisted of 80,000 men, commanded by Marshal Masséna, and divided into three corps, under the orders of Marshal Ney, and Generals Junot and Regnier. The two first had united in the neighbourhood of Salamanca, and occupied the

173

country between the Douro and the Tagus. The third was in Estremadura, opposite to the frontier of Alentejo, its right communicating at Alcantara with the left of Marshal Ney's corps. A fourth body of reserve was to assemble at Valladolid, under the orders of General Drouet, to reinforce or sustain the invading army in case of need.

The army of Lord Wellington, which was opposed to that of Masséna, amounted to 30,000 English, and 30,000 Portuguese. The Regency of Portugal had, besides, 15,000 regular troops under arms, divers flying corps, commanded either by native or English officers, and levies in mass, known by the name of *Ordenança*, which the English estimated only at 45,000 men, but which, in case of invasion, really consisted of the whole population of Portugal in arms. They were animated against the French by patriotism, by hatred, by revenge, and by the still fresh recollection of the evils they had suffered the two preceding years, during the expedition of General Junot and Marshal Soult, unsuccessful as they were.

The undisciplined bands of natives did incalculable mischief to the French, while fighting for their homes in the passes of their native mountains, where they derived great superiority from their numbers and their local knowledge; but they were useless out of their own districts, for which reason the regular Anglo-Portuguese army under Lord Wellington, notwithstanding all the provocations of the French, never quitted the defensive line it occupied on the frontiers of Portugal, north and south of the Tagus. Besides, the English general was afraid at that time to give battle in the plains of Salamanca, where his enemy could bring against him numerous and formidable cavalry.

After the taking of Ciudad Rodrigo, the French passed the Coa, drove in the English outposts, invested Almeida on the frontiers of Portugal, which they gained by capitulation on the 27th August, thirteen days after the trenches were opened.

General Regnier's division quitted Spanish Estremadura, crossed the Tagus at Alcantara, and concentrated itself with the two other French corps in the neighbourhood of Almeida. The English corps which was opposed to that of General Regnier, towards Elvas and Portalegre, by a correspondent movement crossed the Tagus at Villa Velha, and the whole army of Lord Wellington retired by the left bank of the Mondego to the inexpugnable position of the Sierra de Murcella, behind the Alva.

On the 15th September the French army quitted the neighbourhood of Almeida, entered the valley watered by the Mondego, crossed that river at Celorico, and re-crossed it afterwards at the bridge of Fornos; Marshal Masséna led his army along the right bank of the Mondego, with the intention of seizing Coimbra by a rapid march, believing that the English, who were upon the opposite bank, had left it unprotected.

On the 21st the French reached Vizeu, where they were obliged to wait two whole days for their artillery, which had been delayed by the state of the roads, and by the attacks of the Portuguese militia. On the 24th their advanced guard found the English outposts placed on the opposite bank of the Dao, and drove them in after having repaired the bridges, which had been broken down. In order to defend the defiles in the mountains leading to Coimbra, Lord Wellington had caused his army to cross over from the left to the right bank of the Mondego; in his first position in the Sierra de Murcella he had left but a single brigade of infantry, and a division of cavalry.

The French corps arrived successively on the 25th and the 26th, at the foot of the Sierra de Busaco, the summit of which was occupied by the Anglo-Portuguese army; on the 27th, at six o'clock in the morning, they marched in column against that army by the two roads leading to Coimbra, by the village of San Antonio de Cantaro, and by the convent of Busaco; these roads were broken up in different places, and defended by artillery; the hill by which they passed is besides thick set with steep rocks, and it is extremely difficult of access.

The French column, which attacked the English right, advanced with intrepidity, notwithstanding the fire of their artillery and their light infantry; it reached the top of the hill with considerable loss. It began to form in line with great coolness and the most perfect regularity, when it was attacked anew by a superior force and obliged to retire; it rallied soon after, made a second attack, and was again repulsed. The French battalions who were advancing against the convent of Busaco, where the left and centre of the English met, were likewise repulsed just before they reached that point, leaving General Simon, who had been struck by two balls during the charge, and a good number of wounded officers and soldiers, on the height.

The English and Portuguese occupied a position on the summit of the hills, which formed part of a circle whose two extremities embraced the ground over which the French were advancing; the Allied army, seeing their least movements from above, had time to unite its forces in proper points to receive them, which circumstance principally contributed to the advantage it gained. The French lost 1,800 men in their attack, and they had nearly 3,000 wounded; the English and Portuguese had only 1,235 men disabled from fighting.

Marshal Masséna judged it impossible to attack Lord Wellington's position in front, and therefore resolved to turn it: he kept up the battle till night by his riflemen, and sent a body of troops along the road between Mortagao and Oporto; in consequence of which movement the English and Portuguese abandoned their positions on the mountains of Busaco.

The French entered Coimbra on the 1st October,

continued their road, and on the 12th, after eleven days of forced marches, in the midst of rains, they reached Alenquer, nine leagues from Lisbon. They seemed now on the point of reaching the farthest extremity of Portugal, and already looked upon that country as a certain conquest. Imagining that the English were preparing to reimbark, they relied upon reaching them in a very few days, forcing them to give battle in the confusion attendant on their departure, and overwhelming them with superior forces.

But some reconnoitring parties, sent out in different directions, found Lord Wellington's army entrenched in a position which it was impossible either to attack or to turn, between the sea and the Tagus, on the chain of mountains which extend from Alhandra to Torres Vedras, and the mouth of the Sisandro, and run back in the direction of Mafra.

Passes already strong by nature, were rendered more difficult by formidable artillery planted at short distances; numerous places of defence had been most skilfully constructed, whence death could be dispensed without incurring any risk. Silence, calmness, and good order reigned in all the English and Portuguese posts, over the whole breadth of the advanced peninsula in which Lisbon is situated, as if it had been one fortified place. Gun boats stationed on the Tagus flanked the position on the right, and a ball from one of them killed General Saint-Croix on the very first day, as he went up an eminence to make observations.

The French sought, in vain, to provoke Lord Wellington to come out and give them battle. That modern Fabius remained immovable in his lines, and coolly contemplated his enemies below him, from the top of his high rocks. Wisely economical of the blood of his soldiers, he refused to shed it for his personal glory, or to risk the fate of the country he had undertaken to defend on the event of a single battle. It was to the vengeance of the invaded people that he meant to leave the French; by following a plan well and deeply calculated, he made them struggle with hunger and disease, the eternal scourges of conquering armies when they are not called upon and seconded by the wishes of the nation they invade.

By the advice of Lord Wellington, and the orders of the Regency of Portugal, the whole population of the valley of the Mondego, and that of the northern bank of the Tagus had universally quitted their dwellings. The men in the flower of their age had retired to the mountains with nothing but their cattle and their arms, and at the approach of the French, an immense crowd of old men, women, and children, priests and nuns, were seen at once destroying their own resources in order to cut off those of the French, and retiring towards Lisbon to claim the protection of the English army.

The charity of different convents, enlightened by patriotism and seconded by numerous alms, furnished these voluntary exiles with the means of subsistence. In the streets, in the squares, and without the walls of the town, behind the entrenched positions of the English, a peaceful camp had been formed for them, almost as useful to the cause of Portugal as that of the warriors destined to defend the country in arms.

In their rapid march between Almeida and Alenquer the French, to use their own expressions, had found 'only deserted towns and villages; the mills were destroyed, the wine casks stove in the streets, the corn burned, and even the furniture broken. They had seen neither horse, nor mule, nor ass, nor cow, nor goat.'* They fed upon the beasts of burthen which carried their baggage and biscuit with which they had been served for a limited number of days before

*See the Account of Transactions in Portugal in the Moniteur of the 30th November, 1810.

178

they entered Portugal, for they had relied on obtaining by victory the immense resources of one of the most commercial capitals in Europe.

Unexpectedly stopped at the very moment when they thought themselves sure of attaining the object of their labours, they found themselves reduced to live upon what the soldiers could individually procure, when chance, necessity, their natural activity, and the habits of the wandering and warlike life they had so long led, taught them to discover victuals buried by the peasants in secret places, to prevent their enjoying them.

The French were surrounded on all sides, and their communications interrupted by flying corps even before they arrived before the lines of Torres Vedras. The city of Coimbra, where they had left a garrison, different commissariats to form magazines, and their sick and wounded to the number of five thousand men, had been retaken on the 7th by some Portuguese militia, as well as other French posts on the right bank of the Mondego.

The corps commanded by the Portuguese generals Sylveira and Bacellar and the militia of Colonels Trant, Miller, Wilson, and Grant had occupied the roads by which Masséna's army expected its convoys of provisions and ammunition. The right flank of that army was besides teased and harassed by sorties from the Portuguese garrisons of Peniche, Ourem, and Obidos: the armed peasants joined themselves to the militia, in order to attack the detachments and foragers of the French, who purchased their daily bread by daily losses.

While this war in detail was carried on against the flanks and rear, with all the activity revenge and exasperated national hatred could inspire, the English, always on their guard within the lines, enjoyed the greatest tranquillity and did not lose a single man; their videttes never fired upon those of the French, and there was no attempt made by the outposts of either party to provoke or weary each other by feigned attacks. This profound calmness, which reigned in front of the two armies in presence of each other, was the result of that kind of tacit agreement which usually takes place between troops who have neither hatred nor passion to gratify, even when actually engaged in battle, because they are but indirectly interested in the cause they defend.

The French remained at the foot of the lines of Torres Vedras, suffering with patience all the privations they were enduring, in hopes of reducing their enemies to despair. They doubted not but that the immense crowd of inhabitants of every age and sex, which they had pressed forward before them and shut up with the population of the capital in a narrow and sterile piece of ground, would starve the enemy's army, and force it either to reembark or to fight; but the English and Portuguese had the broad ocean behind them, and their swift and numerous ships freely communicated with both hemispheres. Provisions were at first sent from England and Brazil, and numerous trading fleets, attracted by the hope of gain, came afterwards to bring supplies from Africa and America, and the provinces of Spain and Portugal not yet invaded soon furnished nearer resources in great abundance.

The French, weakened by daily losses, and by sickness, in consequence of the scarcity of provisions and inactivity, soon found themselves in the very situation to which they were in hopes of reducing their enemies.

Abrantes and the river Zezere kept the detachments, which attempted to forage in the rear towards Upper Estremadura, in check; and the Tagus, all the bridges over which had been broken down, separated them to the left from Lower Estremadura and Alentejo; these provinces had hitherto been untouched, and their proximity tended to increase the desire of the French, to possess them in the midst of their extreme distress. Among others, they threatened the inhabitants of Chamusca, a little town situated on the opposite bank of the river, with destroying their dwellings if they did not bring in their boats. The only answer returned by the fishermen to whom the boats belonged was to set the boats on fire. The country immediately rose in arms, and the English sent a division of infantry and another of cavalry to the south side of the Tagus, in order to oppose the designs of the French. Lord Wellington had received a reinforcement of ten thousand Spaniards under the Marquis Romana, and he employed a number of seamen from the English fleet in serving the heavy guns; which allowed him to detach divisions to guard the right bank of the Tagus, without weakening his lines.

After remaining above a month before the lines of Torres Vedras, between Villa Franca, Sobral Villa-Nueva, Otta, and Aleventre, the French were on the point of a total want of provisions. They broke up their camp during the night between the 14th and 15th November, and began to retreat in order to take up their position at Santarem behind Rio Major. The good order and silence that they observed at their departure were such that the English videttes did not perceive the absence of the French posts and videttes which were opposed to them till the next day.

The English sent considerable reinforcements to their troops on the southern bank of the Tagus, being fearful lest the new movement of the French should have been undertaken in order to cross that river, and their army left its lines, followed the traces of the French, and on the 19th advanced in column to the Rio Major opposite to Santarem, appearing to threaten to force the position of the French. Lord Wellington established his headquarters at Cartaxo, placing his advanced posts on the right bank of the Rio Major between that river and the lines of Torres Vedras, so as to be prepared to retire to them if the French should have returned to attack him with a superior force.

181

The town of Santarem is situated on the summit of a chain of high and nearly perpendicular hills, before which there is another chain of hills a little lower, on which the first line of the French was extended; at the foot of these hills runs the Rio Major, and a little farther on the Tagus. The English had to cross a kind of wide morass by two causeways, which as well as the bridge were completely commanded by the artillery.

Marshal Masséna had ably chosen and fortified the position of Santarem, in hopes of being able, with a small body of troops, to keep the English upon the Rio Major in check, and without running any risk to extend his cantonments as far as the river Zezere, over which he caused two bridges to be thrown. He occupied both banks of it by a division of infantry, in order to watch Abrantes and to protect the detachments which were sent to forage in Upper Estremadura. He hoped also to maintain a communication with Spain by way of Thomar, until reinforcements which he hoped for and which were indispensable to enable him to continue his operations after the losses he had sustained should arrive and drive the Portuguese militia from the posts they had carried on the roads, in the valley of the Mondego.

The reserve under General Drouet had left Valladolid on the 12th October, and was advancing towards the frontiers of Portugal; and General Gardanne's division, which had remained in garrison in the towns of Ciudad-Rodrigo and Almeida, had also set out to join Marshal Masséna's army. On the 14th November, being arrived within a few leagues of the first French posts, that corps had suddenly fallen back towards the Spanish frontiers. It was led into an error concerning the situation of affairs by the numerous Portuguese militia which had harassed it since its entrance into Portugal, and which had even carried off its advanced guard. Gardanne's division fell back upon General

Drouet's corps, with which it re-entered Portugal in the month of December.

General Drouet's corps took the road towards the valley of the Mondego, and joined Marshal Masséna's army after having dispersed the militia without destroying it, which was always the case, for the Portuguese General Sylveira returned at the end of the month to attack Claparède's division, which had been left at Trancoso and Pinhel in the district of the Coa in order to maintain the communication between the army of Portugal with Spain. General Claparède rallied his division, beat General Sylveira and pursued him to the Duero; but he was soon forced back to Trancoso and Guarda, by other bodies of militia under the Portuguese General Bacellar, and Colonel Wilson, who fell upon his flank and rear at Castro Diaro and upon the Pavio.

The Portuguese militia never attacking any but the weak parts of the army, that is, the advanced guards, rearguards, detachments, small garrisons, or single corps, did a great deal of mischief; and it was impossible to destroy it on account of its number and its perfect knowledge of the country. General Drouet arrived at Leyria, and with the rest of the French army, occupied the country extending between the sea and the Tagus, towards Punhete and Santarem. Marshal Masséna was building a great number of boats at Punhete in order to throw bridges over the Tagus; it was a difficult undertaking in a country deserted by its inhabitants, and which besides possessed but few resources at any time. The English corps occupying Mugem, Almerin, Chamusca, and San Brito, on the opposite bank, saw all these preparatives and constructed strong batteries on their own side.

It was as important to the English to prevent the French from crossing the river as it was to these latter to effect it; for the fate of Portugal and the ultimate success of either party then appeared to depend upon it. If Marshal Masséna had

183

effected the crossing of the river, the English would have been obliged to divide their forces and weaken themselves by extending their lines on each side of its banks. The positions of Torres Vedras, being less carefully guarded and not having in that case a sufficient number of men to defend them, might have been carried by a French corps advancing from Leyria upon Lisbon at the expense of the sacrifice of several thousand men. If, on the contrary, the English had concentrated all their troops in the lines of Torres Vedras, the French would have gone down the Tagus after having crossed it, and have seized the peninsula in which the towns of Palmela and Setuval are situated; from the extremity of that peninsula they might have made themselves masters of the course of the Tagus and have starved Lisbon; in short, from the heights of Almada opposite to that capital, they might have bombarded it.

On the 9th January Marshals Soult and Mortier arrived with all the disposable troops of the Andalusian army, in hopes of raising the sieges of Badajos and Elvas, and forcing Lord Wellington to divide his troops to defend that part of the Portuguese frontier, and thus to co-operate with Marshal Masséna. On the news of their approach towards the frontiers of Alentejo, the English sent fresh troops under the command of Generals Hill and Beresford, to the south of the Tagus, and the inhabitants of that part of the country made ready to desert it, in order to famish the French according to the defensive system which Lord Wellington had followed on the left bank of the river with success.

The Marquis de la Romana sent General Mendizabal to the assistance of Badajos with the 10,000 Spaniards which he had brought to the lines of Torres Vedras. The Marquis was seized with the illness of which he died on the 24th January at Cartaxo, deeply regretted by the Spaniards and the English, esteemed by his enemies for never having despaired of his country's cause, and for having always kept up the war even in the midst of defeat with an activity and perseverance which seem usually to belong only to the conquering party. Marshals Soult and Mortier took Olivença on the 23rd January: and afterwards on the 19th February they crossed the Gevora and the Guadiana, invested Badajos, and surprised and cut to pieces General Mendizabal's Spanish army in its camp under the walls of that place.

Meantime Marshal Masséna's army had consumed all the provisions of the country it occupied on the right bank of the Tagus, and its foragers had to extend their excursions to twenty miles round. A good part of the army was always employed in procuring sustenance for the rest, and it was only by severe daily losses that they obtained even a daily and precarious subsistence.

General Junot having learned that the English had formed a magazine of corn and wine at Rio Major, set out to seize it at the head of two regiments of cavalry and some infantry belonging to his own corps. The English retired in good time, and the general was wounded in a slight skirmish which took place between his advanced-guard and the English rear. The cavalry, which ought to be, in a manner, the eyes and the hands of a great army, being destined to procure and to keep its provisions, was a burthen to the French, from its number, on account of the difficulty of providing for it, and besides it was often useless in a mountainous country intersected by narrow passes and continually harassed by an innumerable militia and peasantry.

The irritation and hatred of the inhabitants of the country increased with the continuance of the war, on account of the privations they endured. Even the most timid peasants, who had only fled to the mountains in hopes of living in peace, were driven from their retreats by despair and hunger. They descended into the valleys, lay in ambush on the roads, and awaited the French in difficult passes to rob them of the very provisions which they had procured by

185

plunder. A peasant in the neighbourhood of Thomar had chosen, as his place of retreat, a cavern near the town, and during the month of February he had, with his own hand, killed more than thirty Frenchmen whom he contrived to surprise separately, and he had carried off nearly fifty horses and mules.

The guerrillas in Spain had increased very much in boldness since so large a part of the French forces had been employed in Portugal. The Spanish chiefs, who seven months before had scarcely two or three hundred men under their command, were now at the head of formidable divisions, and often carried off the convoys of ammunition and victuals destined for the French army in Portugal. These convoys had to pass through two hundred leagues of an enemy's country in arms against them, before they could reach their destination. These convoys were composed of muleteers put in requisition in the south of France, and of Spanish peasants who very unwillingly exposed themselves to the almost certain danger of being put to death, or of losing their mules. These peasants fled the moment they found an opportunity, or gave notice beforehand to the guerrillas, that they might be spared in their attacks: the least negligence on the part of the escorts would have deprived the army of provisions.

By the beginning of March Marshal Masséna had succeeded in constructing two hundred boats, and all his preparations were finished; but he could not attempt to cross the Tagus without fresh reinforcements; and Marshals Soult and Mortier could give him no effectual assistance by advancing towards the Tagus, till after the reduction of Badajos, which still held out.

Lord Wellington's army had not suffered any considerable loss since the beginning of the campaign: it had recently received reinforcements from England, and amounted to near 40,000 English, without counting the

Portuguese regular troops which had been considerably augmented, and were improved by discipline and experience. That of Marshal Masséna, on the contrary, had for seven months suffered daily losses by partial attacks of the Portuguese militia, by want of provisions, and by sickness; and it was reduced to one-half the number it contained on its entrance into Portugal.

Such was the situation of the French in that country at the beginning of the month of March, when a convoy of biscuit, which they expected from France, was taken by the Spanish partisans. On the eve of a total want of food, they were now forced to think of retreating, and they quitted Portugal after a campaign of seven months, without having fought a single pitched battle, but yielding to the perseverance of the English chief in following a plan by which he had constantly deprived his enemy of every chance of success, by preventing him from finding a single opportunity of fighting.

On the 4th the sick, the wounded, and the baggage set out on a number of sumpter cattle, and on the 5th the army began its retreat. The care of the rearguard was entrusted to Marshal Ney, who advanced with his corps from Leyria to Muliano, to threaten the flanks of the English army by that offensive demonstration, and to force it to remain stationary, while the other French corps got forwards.

On the 10th the French reached Pombal; their rearguard stopped the English advanced guard for nearly the whole day of the 11th before that town; they abandoned it towards evening, and during the night, they retired to a strong position in advance from the defile of Redinha on the Adanços. They repassed the defile on the approach of the English under the protection of the artillery, which was placed on the neighbouring heights, and played on the enemy's advanced guard. The French rearguard formed itself in battle array, behind the defile of Redinha, and

187

retired upon the main body of the army which was awaiting it in the position of Condeixa.

The skill of the French, says an English narrator,* displayed itself every moment; they did not allow a single advantage offered by the ground to escape. Their rearguard never abandoned a position they had to defend, till they had been completely turned, and then it was only to take up another and defend itself anew. The French columns retired slowly upon a central point in a chosen position, where they met in a body to rest, to resist the enemy, to repulse them, and then renew their march. Marshal Ney covered the retreat with some chosen corps, while Marshal Masséna directed the march of the body of the army, and was always ready to support the rearguard in case of need. 'The talents of that great captain,' says the English Military Journal,** 'never appeared so conspicuously; nothing can equal the skill he then displayed.'

On the 15th the French took up their position on the Ceira, leaving an advance guard at the village of Foz de Aronce, where there was a pretty sharp engagement; on the 16th they destroyed the bridge over the Ceira, and quitted their position on the 17th, in order to retire behind the Alva. The main army of the English stopped upon the Alva to wait for provisions; and as far as Guarda the French were only followed by light troops, Portuguese militia, and the natives of the country, who incessantly harassed them with the greatest animosity, never giving any quarter to laggers, or the wounded who happened to fall into their hands.

The want of subsistence forced the French to hasten their march: on quitting Portugal, as on entering it, the French found nothing but deserted towns and empty habitations

*History of Europe, Edinburgh Annual Register, Vol. IV. 1811, p. 257.
**Military Chronicle, Vol. II p. 405.

where there were no provisions. Exasperated by fatigue and privations, the soldiers gave themselves up to all kinds of excesses, and set fire to the villages and even the towns. In their greedy searches, they profaned the churches by spoiling them of their ornaments, violated the tombs, dispersed the relics, revenging themselves on the ashes of the dead, instead of the living, whom they could not reach. The French remained at Guarda till the 28th; they left that town on the approach of the English, to take up the strong position of Ruivinha; they defended the ford of Rapoula de Coa, during the whole of the 3rd and 4th, with some advantage, and re-passed the Portuguese frontier leaving a weak garrison in Almeida.

The system of defence, which reduced Marshal Masséna's army to the necessity of leaving Portugal after having invaded it, was the same as that of the Spaniards: every nation which is inspired by true patriotism may employ it with equal success.

It consists in avoiding pitched battles, in forcing a large army to divide itself in order to fight those corps in detail which are palsied for want of union. Or, if it remains collected in one place, to exhaust it by depriving it of all means of procuring subsistence and ammunition, which becomes the more easy as it is the more numerous and more removed by its own successes from the country whence it should draw its resources.

In the great military states in the centre of Europe, where the nation interests itself but little in the quarrels of the government, a battle gained, or simply the occupation of a country, gave the French provisions in abundance, ammunition, horses, arms, and even soldiers; and one might say of their army what Virgil says of Fame, '*vires acquirit eundo*', its strength gathered as it went.

In Spain and Portugal, on the contrary, the forces of the French diminished as they advanced, from the necessity of

189

detaching numerous corps to oppose the population of the country, to procure subsistence, and to keep up distant communications; and their army soon found itself reduced, even after victory, to the situation of the lion in the fable who wounded himself with his own claws in vain efforts to destroy the flies who tormented and followed him wherever he went.

Europe ought never to forget that Spain maintained the burden of the immense power of the Emperor Napoleon almost alone for upwards of five years. Victorious in Italy, on the Danube, on the Elbe, and on the Niemen, he had subjected or attached to his fortunes the greater part of Europe. By uniting the conquerors and the conquered under the same banners, he had in a manner converted his enemies into his companions in arms. The Italians, the Poles, the Swiss, the Dutch, the Saxons, the Bavarians, and all the warlike tribes of the Confederation of the Rhine, mingled in the ranks of the French, emulous of their glory, took delight in proving to them in their battles, that like them they could despise danger and death.

The great powers situated to the north and east of Europe, who, notwithstanding their misfortunes, had still strength enough to struggle, were apparently palsied by the name of Napoleon's power. He distributed kingdoms to his companions in arms throughout Europe, as he did govern-ments in France to his creatures, and the name and author-ity of king had come to be looked upon as nothing more than a step of military rank in his army.

When hostilities first commenced in Spain in 1808, the French army had invaded Portugal without striking a blow; they occupied Madrid, the centre of Spain, and had seized several fortresses by stratagem. The flower of the Spanish troops was detained with the French forces in Germany and in Portugal: those which remained in Spain could not then distinguish between the authority of the French, and the wishes of the Kings Charles IV or Ferdinand VII.

When the Emperor Napoleon gave his brother to Spain as a king, and kept the two sovereigns prisoners in France, he was in hopes that he would have to do with a feeble nation, without energy, which, once deprived of its chiefs, would prefer the government of a stranger to the scourge of war in the very heart of the country. Europe herself believed along with the Emperor Napoleon that the Spaniards were to be subdued without a struggle.

During these five years that the war had lasted the French had gained ten pitched battles successively, they had taken almost every strong place, but nevertheless they had not secured the durable possession of a single province. Spain had been in a manner reduced to Cadiz, as Portugal was to Lisbon. But though the French had been able to take those towns, even then the fate of the Peninsula would not have been decided. Whilst the French armies lay under the walls of Cadiz and Lisbon the Spanish partisans were making incursions to the gates of Thoulouse, in the very heart of France.

The Spaniards, as a nation, were animated by one and the same feeling, love of independence, and abhorrence of strangers who would have humbled their national pride by imposing a government upon them. It was neither armies nor fortresses that were to be conquered in Spain, but that one, yet multiplied sentiment which filled the whole people. It was the inmost soul of each and every one that resisted the blow – that entrenchment which neither ball nor bayonet could reach.

Since these memoirs were written we have seen, first the Muscovite and since the Prussian people, give to the north of Europe proofs of devotion to their country similar, in many respects, to that which has illustrated the Spaniards and Russia, Prussia, and Spain were early delivered from the common enemy. These events have changed the face of Europe; they demonstrate as fully as the long and noble resistance of the Spanish people, that the real strength of states does not consist so much in the number and strength of their regular armies, as in that religious, patriotic, or political feeling which is alone powerful enough to interest every individual of a nation in the public cause as if it were his own.